Praise for *Writing for the Cut*

"Refreshing and thought provoking. This is the first book I've encountered that profoundly illuminates the connection between screenwriting and editing. An essential handbook for filmmakers who aspire to deepen their craft. A wonderfully inspiring read!" —**Lisa Gunning**, editor, *Seven Psychopaths*, *Nowhere Boy*

"Full of great ideas, quotes, examples, and practical exercises to improve your script so it translates cinematically into a well-edited movie. Essential reading." —**Eddie Hamilton**, editor, *Mission: Impossible—Fallout*, *Kickass*

"Extraordinary and provocative . . . Loftin expresses a unique take on screenwriting using a wide range of sources (Ralf Rosenblum, Walter Murch, and Steven Johnson). As a film editor turned screenwriter, I find his point of view illuminating." —**David Peoples**, writer, *Unforgiven*; co-writer, *Blade Runner*

"Combining a heartfelt love of film with a keen experimenter's drive to roll up some sleeves and get amongst the editing software, Loftin takes us on a romp through the shaping of screen stories that delights and inspires." —**Warren Coleman**, writer, co-director, *Happy Feet*

"A picture is worth a thousand words, but then a word can be worth a thousand pictures. Greg Loftin's excellent book will help filmmakers navigate the often tricky, sometimes treacherous path from the chrysalis of the screenplay to the butterfly of the finished film." —**Walter Murch**, editor, *The Conversation*, *Apocalypse Now*, *The English Patient*, *Return to Oz*

"A fascinating new way to teach the art and craft of screenwriting. With practical advice, exercises, and examples from current and classic films, *Writing for the Cut* lets a writer envision how a scene will play out on the screen, then gives them new tools to write that scene in a more vivid and cinematic way." —**Victoria Lucas**, development and production executive; Fellow, Hanson Film Institute at the University of Arizona; independent producer

"Greg Loftin has written a unique, informational book that will teach you, the writer, how to think differently about crafting your script. You'll learn how to embed your editing ideas without stepping on your editor's toes. It's a book loaded with 'a-ha!' moments." —**Forris Day Jr.**, host, "Rolling Tape" video podcast; cohost, "Get Real: Indie Filmmakers" p

"Tapping into the insight of editors and many of cinema's most authoritative figures, Greg provides an indispensable manual for any student or practicing screenwriter, film editor, or director!" —**Mick Audsley**, editor, *Harry Potter and the Goblet of Fire, Everest*

"Loftin does a great job showing how the impact of cut can be represented in the script. He also provides exercises that bring the cut to the page. Highly recommended!" —**Ly Bolia**, associate professor, Georgia State University

"Don't leave it all up to a director, cinematographer, or editor you've never met to understand and tell your story. This book contains history, techniques, and fun exercises that any screenwriter can use. It digs deep into the overlapping arts of writing and editing, giving you what you need: an understanding of visual storytelling!" —**Carl King**, writer / director, *The Oracle of Outer Space*

"Successfully bridges the information gap between screenwriter and film editor, two artists who might work on the same project but never meet. A screenplay is words on paper, while film is moving images bringing those words to life (and art), so finesse is required in crafting a film story—what Loftin calls 'capturing the dance of the edit in the writing.' Teachers of advanced screenwriting should include this book on their required reading list." —**Mary J. Schirmer**, screenwriter; script consultant; editor; instructor

"Loftin knows how integral and indispensable editing is to the filmmaking process. A wonderful toolkit and read." —**Dave Watson**, author, *Walkabout Undone*; editor, Movies Matter

"Innovative . . . your writing will become less literary and more visual. Earn your place among the artists and craftspeople who actually make movies! After reading this book, I found half a dozen moments in my current script where writing for the cut strengthened what was on the page." —**Murray Suid**, screenwriter, *Summer of the Flying Saucer*; coauthor (with James Morrow), *Moviemaking Illustrated*

"Essential. Loftin looks at what the initiators of the filmmaking process, the writers, can learn from the people who finish it, the editors. His central argument—that screenwriters are not writers like any others, and need to think about the art form that is cinema as an integral part of their process—is rare enough to be thought provoking, and the practical advice that is given throughout the book makes this opus utterly indispensable to anyone eager to make a truly cinematic screenplay." —**Baptiste Charles**, raindance.org; writer / producer, Bubble Wrap Productions

Writing for the Cut

Shaping Your Script for Cinema

GREG LOFTIN

MICHAEL WIESE PRODUCTIONS

Published by Michael Wiese Productions
12400 Ventura Blvd. #1111
Studio City, CA 91604
(818) 379-8799, (818) 986-3408 (FAX)
mw@mwp.com
www.mwp.com

This book was set in
Garamond Premier Pro,
Bebas, and DIN

Cover design by Johnny Ink
johnnyink.com
Interior design by Debbie Berne
Copyediting by Ross Plotkin
Printed by McNaughton & Gunn

Manufactured in the United States of America

Library of Congress Cataloging-in-Publication Data

Names: Loftin, Greg, author.
Title: Writing for the cut : shaping your script for cinema.
Description: Studio City, CA: Michael Wiese Productions, [2019] | Includes bibliographical references.
Identifiers: LCCN 2018043415 | ISBN 9781615933006
Subjects: LCSH: Motion picture authorship.
Classification: LCC PN1996 .L64 2019 | DDC 808.2/3—dc23
LC record available at https://lccn.loc.gov/2018043415

First Printing: June 2019

Printed on Recycled Stock

I started dating June Mong around the same time I began my research.
For a while, I was in a kind of delirium.
We were married before I even got to Chapter 2.
June is everywhere in this book.

CONTENTS

ACKNOWLEDGMENTS

I want to say a special thanks to film editor-director Lisa Gunning; it was her stimulating conversation that got me so fired up at the start of my research. I also want to thank director Matt Mitchell for allowing me to follow the entire journey of his horror screenplay *It Never Sleeps* as it went out on location, was captured on film, and stitched together in the edit suite. And so my thanks also to Richard Hughes for not throwing me out of the edit suite, and for sharing his thoughts as he cut the movie.

This book grew out of my PhD, so a big thanks goes to my supervisor Sam North at Exeter University for all his critical advice and enthusiasm over the years. Thanks also to Prof Lizzie Jackson who saw there might be a researcher in the boy, and to my work-family at Ravensbourne University London for their generosity and critical support.

For pitching in and helping in so many ways, I want to thank my whip-smart friends Steve Mullins, Sabine Stork, Snowden Flood, Jon Puleston, Katie Aidley, David Wigram, and Matt Pritchard.

Thank you to my publisher Michael Wiese for believing this thing had legs, and to Ken Lee for his timely dig in the ribs. Thank you Ana Goncalves for translating *City of God* for me.

ABOUT THIS BOOK

This book helps you put the editing jig into your screen stories. The principles discussed here apply to all screens and all stories. However, I do focus on movie screenplays for several reasons; they're bespoke, they're high end, they tell big stories, and they're fiendishly hard to write.

In these pages, you'll find lots of film-editing strategies that will transport your writing from the word to the moving image. All of them shake out from one central idea: juxtaposition is the motor of film storytelling.

If you follow this book to the end, do the exercises, adopt some of these strategies, you'll never stare at a blank page again. Your creativity will bloom, and your output will surge from snail to cheetah as you enter the editor's world of rapid storytelling.

Who's it for?

All those writing for the screen, from students to teachers to professional screenwriters. Also producers, directors, advertising creatives, and novelists with movies in their heads.

About this book and me

I've been writing scripts for maybe twenty years or so. In 2007, I wrote and directed my first feature film. It's called *Saxon* and it was made with the love and support of friends and family. And a second mortgage. I want to make more, and better films, and I'd like someone else to pay next time.

I think about story a lot. And that's part of my day job too. I'm course leader for a university program in Editing and Postproduction. Whenever I talk to my editing students about story structure, I point them to screenwriting manuals. They're simply the best books on the subject. Then about five years ago a thought struck me: What if we flipped it the other way? What could screenwriters learn from film editors about storytelling?

It seemed like an obvious question, but when I cast around for books and articles on the subject, I was surprised at how little there was. This was the starting point of my Ph.D.

When I began my research, it felt like I'd entered a secret world. Wearing my newly discovered "for the cut" spectacles, I started to read lots of screenplays that had been made into movies, and everywhere I looked I found film-editing shapes in the writing. I marveled at this at the time, but now I've come to understand all professional writers *write for the cut*.

I also devoured editing and screenwriting manuals. Although I found some that made connections between screenwriting and production processes, the only manual entirely devoted to the subject is Margaret Mehring's *The Screenplay: A Blend of Film Form and Content*. This is an excellent book, and although written in the analog world of the 1980s, much of it is still highly relevant.

The three Soviet filmmaker-theorists Kuleshov, Pudovkin, and Eisenstein are a big inspiration for this book. They are the true pioneers of the cut, and they wrote volumes on the subject.

Taking his cue from the Soviets, writer-director David Mamet is probably one of the greatest advocates of the cut. In his book *On Directing Film*, he underscores again and again how the cut should tell the film story: "Let the cut tell the story. Because otherwise you have not got dramatic action, you have narration."

The other major influence here is three-time Oscar-winning editor and sound designer Walter Murch. He is a unique authority on editing, and has written a seminal book and numerous articles on his craft.

I decided early in my research that if I was going to do this job well, I needed to talk to some great movie editors. I interviewed ten, and they have between them over 200 feature film credits. If we gave each a single credit, we'd include: *Lawrence of Arabia* (Anne Coates), *Taxi Driver* (Tom Rolf), *Apocalypse Now* (Walter Murch), *High Fidelity* (Mick Audsley), *The Diving Bell and the Butterfly* (Juliette Welfling), *Slumdog Millionaire* (Chris Dickens), *Still Alice* (Nicolas Chaudeurge), *Nowhere Boy* (Lisa Gunning), *Baby Driver* (Paul Machliss), and *Mission: Impossible — Fallout* (Eddie Hamilton).

In this book, I have had to be quite cautious in my use of quotes from editors; this has everything to do with the commercially sensitive nature of their profession. Editors are often referred to as "humble backroom folk." This is partly true, but they are also cautious and cunning. Their profession makes them so. Editors are engaged in an "invisible craft," and they themselves must wear the cloak of invisibility. Editors can't talk freely about the movies they've worked on; any mention of "fixing" problems with the script, performance, or direction could be both damaging at the box office, and to their professional relationships. Few editors will even lay claim to the title "storyteller." This partly explains why their profession is still largely shrouded in mystery. It also explains why I've occasionally anonymized and paraphrased some of their comments here. When not otherwise credited, quotes come from personal interviews.

Three more things before we start . . .

1. This book looks at one craft through the lens of another. Although it touches on some of the traditional territory of screenwriting manuals — genre, character, structure,

and dialogue — the emphasis here is on delivering practical tools to help you write your story the way an editor cuts a film.

2. The screenwriter tells the story in the script, and then the director tells the story again on the shoot. The editor tells the story a third time in the suite. It should be understood that this final "telling" of the story is quite complex: it is the outcome of the creative dialogue between director and editor. And it is more than the sum of all that's gone before.

3. There are exercises at the end of many chapters. Some involve slicing and dicing your own screenplay. If you don't have a screenplay, you can use your treatment, and if you don't have one of those — sheesh, get to work!

For some exercises, you'll use editing software. You don't need anything fancy, and it doesn't matter if you've never edited before.

FOREWORD

As a film editor, I have always been aware of the immense gap that exists between page and screen in the filmmaking process. So often a screenplay reads well on the page but fails to translate successfully to the screen.

Why is there such a gulf between the two ends of the filmmaking timeline?

Perhaps because cinematic storytelling—the juxtaposition of imagery and audio—has its own special language.

When successful, the collision of sound and pictures engages the audience with an economy and sophistication that words can rarely achieve. This narrative power is the very heartbeat of cinema.

So how can the screenwriter close the gap and articulate this unique cinematic language on the page? By using the language that is born shot by shot, scene by scene when a film is put together by the film editor and director.

Writing for the Cut shows us exactly how.

Within this extremely succinct volume, Greg gives us an invaluable insight into how to write for the cinema by considering the chronology of filmmaking in reverse.

He provides us with an in-depth understanding of the principles used when cutting a movie and how film "grammar" can inform the screenplay as it is written.

Tapping into the insight of editors and many of cinema's most authoritative figures, Greg provides us with an indispensable manual for any student or practicing screenwriter, film editor or director!

And that's not all . . .

There are detailed analyses of scenes from movies along with writing exercises that free us from the limitations of the screenplay format and take us into the suggestive, dynamic world of the moving image.

Mick Audsley
April 2019

Twelve Monkeys (1995)
Dirty Pretty Things (2002)
Harry Potter and the Goblet of Fire (2005)
Everest (2015)

INTRODUCTION

Here's an action sequence from Alex Garland's screenplay *Ex Machina*.

Ava is an AI robot, and Nathan is her creator.

```
INT. HOUSE/GLASS CORRIDOR — NIGHT
. . . then AVA breaks into a run.
Sprinting in NATHAN'S direction.


EXT. GARDEN — NIGHT
Quiet in the garden.
Soft wind rush.
Moon and stars reflected in the windows of the
house.


INT. HOUSE/GLASS CORRIDOR — NIGHT
AVA impacts NATHAN, and they fly backwards.
```

So Ava is running towards Nathan, they're about to collide, and then — eh? We cut to a quiet garden and contemplate the beauty of the cosmos. Bam! Ava impacts Nathan.

Why did Garland do that? Why did he take us away from a nice action scene to go look at the stars?

The answer is juxtaposition. And juxtaposition is the DNA of cinema.

This book reveals an approach to screenwriting that all the best screenwriters seem to know by instinct. They shape their scripts for the tailor shop where the film is actually made: the edit suite.

We're heading off on a journey into the editor's secret world of storytelling. We'll discover ways this can be wrapped into the writing so your screenplay will jump and jive with the storytelling pulse of the cut.

I call this *writing for the cut.*

Of course, you do need to start this process with a cinema-size story. You might not have one of those right now, but as soon as you understand how the cut tells the story, windows will open onto story worlds you'd never seen before.

Tell the story in images and sounds

Many screenwriting manuals agree a screenplay should tell a story in images and sounds. But virtually none give clear guidance on how the written word can be made to function in the way that images and sounds function for the big screen.

Maybe it's just too obvious — we've all seen thousands of movies, we know they've been edited, and we know that what we're writing should end up looking like one of those. Don't we?

Well some do (great screenwriters) and most don't (the rest of us).

The written word and the moving image are discrete mediums. And the story physics of each are different. All of us know how to write stories, but telling that story for the big screen is a jump to a different world.

Film has native ways of telling stories — it uses a language that has evolved over a hundred years in a dark and secret place.

That place is the edit suite.

Hiding in plain sight

If we want to discover film's native storytelling language, it's right there, in every movie we've ever watched. But we can't see it — or rather, we're not supposed to see it. Editing is often called "the invisible craft" — it succeeds most when it is least seen. The finished film presents a sheer surface to the viewer so we can enjoy the content without getting snagged on the construction.

But if we could break through that sheer surface, what would we see? When the cuts are made visible, we'd see all the screenwriterly shapes that we know and love, but transformed by the dynamics of moving images, light, color, sound, time, motion, rhythm, sequence, and fragment. But for screenwriters, the most striking thing we'd notice is what happens at the cut itself — the narrative pulse of juxtaposition.

Juxtaposition is a kind of magic. Through the collision of images, we ignite fresh ideas in the mind of the viewer. And when we do that, viewers become active partners in the storytelling — they *discover* the story for themselves. Discovering the story, rather than being literally told the story, is what gives us greatest pleasure when we watch a film. The Pixar writer-director Andrew Stanton puts it like this:

> "Good storytelling never gives you four, it gives you two plus two . . . Don't give the audience the answer. Audiences have an unconscious desire to work for their entertainment. They are rewarded with a sense of thrill and delight when they find the answers themselves." (*Screenwriting Expo 5*)

Writing for the cut gives you two plus two. It's an approach that informs your entire script development from the hatching of your story to final-draft screenplay. *Writing for the cut* is a way of writing in images and sounds that will move, fragment, and collide on the big screen. And in the mind of the viewer.

Returning to *Ex Machina*, it's clear that Alex Garland was writing in images with editing in mind. There is a kind of poetry here.

And poetry is our bridge between the world of words and the world of cinema.

For-the-cut strategies

In this book, you will discover how to apply a number of for-the-cut strategies to your writing. All stem from the poetry of the cut:

Substitution splice — magic at the scene break
Split scene break — spill across the cut
Nonlinear shuffle — move the parts around
Ellipsis — don't show don't tell
In medias res — start in the middle
Script-planned montage — poetry in motion
Opening / title sequence — overture
Parallel action — the thrill of cross-cutting
Action scenes — writing the set piece
Suspense — stretching those nerves
Dialogue — another kind of action

The message of this book is a simple one: the cut tells the story. But the cut has a second edge, and this edge has a kind of diagnostic function; it reveals everything that's "wrong" with the movie. Problems with acting, cinematography, and directing are nakedly exposed in the edit suite. These are production problems so screenwriters may think they're off the hook. But here's the thing: the cut is even more brutal in revealing bad dialogue and flaws in the story. In later chapters, we look at this diagnostic property of the cut and explore ways we might simulate at the script stage what goes on in the suite.

Everyone writes for the cut

Whenever I give my twenty-second elevator pitch for *writing for the cut*, most people get it in a blink. Right after the blink, people will say, "But that's obvious," or "But that's what I do."

I think I'm just giving a name to a practice that for many is simply instinctive, particularly amongst director-screenwriters, editor-screenwriters, and all those "mechanics" who have pushed their faces up close to the screen to see how film stories really work.

Editing is far from a passive assembly of jigsaw pieces: it is an active continuation of the storytelling. Quentin Tarantino nails it when he says:

> "The first draft of the script is the first cut of the movie and the final cut of the movie is the last draft of the script." (*The Magic of Movie Editing*)

We're still using a typewriter

Think about the technological marvels of film since it exploded into our world over a hundred years ago. Consider the advances made in cameras, sound recording, film stock, digital acquisition, visual effects, and color grading. Look at the evolution of editing from the cut-and-glue techniques of the silent era to the kind of software editors use today. What about screenwriting technology? We started on a typewriter a hundred years ago, and today we can sit at our shiny computers, open our favorite screenwriting software and . . . oh, we're sitting at a typewriter again.

All aspects of film have been radically transformed by the big shift from analog to digital production. Except the writing bit. We poor screenwriters are still fumbling along, word by word, page by page. Draft after draft. On our own. Sometimes weeping. Screenwriting software is great for doing a certain job. But in many ways, it works against the grain of our creativity: we do not think in linear ways, we do not think like typewriters.

Film stories are all about structure. For each new film story, we're effectively designing a new model. We're in the business of prototyping, a process in which failure is a prerequisite of success. Editors use software that allows them to rapidly compose / play / fail / revise / play again. We screenwriters on the other hand are engaged in a process that guarantees really slow failure: write, write (some years pass), write some more ... show someone ... fail ... rewrite ...

Today, we live in a world of digital plenty, and we can snag free and inexpensive software and start to compose our stories "in the cutting room." We can write in text, gather visual proxies, and rehearse our beats and sequences. We can see the structure of our story, and in some measure, we can prove it for cinema.

Editing software is a magical storytelling tool, this book shows ways to gatecrash the edit suite and enter a world of serendipity.

CHAPTER 1

STUDIO EXILES

Are we writing for cinema, or a notion of cinema? How screenwriters lost their memory of filmmaking

WRITING FOR THE CUT beats a path between writing and making. Every word you write must of necessity be makeable, doable, and speakable. Working alone on our computers in the front room, we can easily lose sight of this. And when we lose sight of this, we'll just carry on writing. Because we don't even know we've stopped writing for cinema.

In the beginning, screenwriters "made" the movies. They worked at film studios and had production constantly in their sights. But the industry changed and we became exiles. The fallout has been mixed.

It's worth spending a moment here to see what we're trying to fix.

Are we writing for cinema or a notion of cinema?

During Hollywood's silent era and well into the talkies, the screenwriter's place of work was the movie studio. At that time, screenwriters needed to have an intimate knowledge of film production crafts. They used a screenplay format called the Continuity Script, which not only presented the film story, but also included the manufacturing instructions (details about camera angles, mise-en-scene, and editing). This generation of screenwriters were versed in the practice of movie making and they were literally writing for the shoot and the cut.

By the 1950s, most of the studio writing departments had disappeared, and screenwriters began writing their stories away from the "factory floor." As part of this shift, a new screenplay format, the Master Scene, became the industry standard. This format removed the burden on screenwriters to include production details (MS, POV, ZOOM IN, etc.) so the writer could focus solely on the story. Now virtually anyone with a great story could write a spec script. And to help them, they could draw on expert advice from a growing library of screenwriting manuals. Manuals from this era right up to the present day play a really important role — in a sense they stand in for studio apprenticeships and film schools. The best of them have redefined our craft and helped us to think about storytelling in truly fresh and original ways.

In a crowded market, all manuals attempt to have a unique voice — a distinctive angle on the craft. But there's one thing they all agreed on: *Do not mention camera angles, camera movements, sound design, or editing. Break this rule and you and your script will go straight to hell in a handcart.* And it's sometimes as emphatic as that. Of course, the authority for this comes from the film industry, and from the Master Scene format itself. At heart, this interdiction is all about respecting the director's vision.

So what's the problem?

Getting rid of all those shot descriptors was surely a good thing. For the reader, scripts became more lucid, immersive, and succinct. For directors and editors, they gained a fuller measure of creative freedom. And for screenwriters, they could finally tell their stories without having to prefigure the shoot. As the famous manual writer Syd Field put it:

> "You don't have to tell the director and cinematographer and film editor how to do their jobs. Your job is to write the screenplay, to give them enough visual information so they can bring those words on the page into life, in full sound and fury." (*Screenplay: The Foundation of Screenwriting*)

And so say all of us. Except that something important got lost.

The manual writers so fiercely upheld the "no camera angles" rule, it became almost taboo to even discuss the shoot and the edit in their books. This is quite weird when you think about it; imagine reading a how-to book for music composers in which discussion of how musical instruments translate your score into sounds was off-limits. By partitioning off the orchestra that plays our stories (cameras, sound, editing, etc.), screenwriting manuals have effectively closed down a vital connection with the behaviors, predispositions, and dynamics of those "instruments." Over time, the "no camera angles" rule has come to foster a nontechnical view of film as a finished, *projected* product. And that's how we can easily end up writing for a notion of cinema.

In this book, we're saying the edit suite is the real destination for our screenplay. *Writing for the cut* says film is a *constructed* product made from fragments. And if we keep that front and center of our storytelling, then we're back in the studio writing department and we're "making" movies.

CHAPTER 2

JUMP

The Kuleshov Effect, and how the cut tells the story:
Getting from the word to the moving image

POETRY IS OUR BRIDGE between the world of words and the world of moving images.

When we watch a film at the cinema, we bathe in projected light, and we lose ourselves in the world of the story. Later when we tell a friend about the film, we will often recall a flowing, linear, and seamless story. That's because we're filling in the gaps. The film has given us two plus two, and we've supplied half of the story from our own imagination.

And so this kind of automatic infill can lead us to write stories that "give the answer." But as soon as we begin to see film as a construction of jumps, jerks, fragments, and collisions, we can better understand what to show and what to hide. Above all, we can focus on what happens at the join. Because what happens at the join is juxtaposition, and juxtaposition is a kind of magic.

The juxtaposition of shots lies at the heart of film storytelling; it sits two contrasting images together, and invites the viewer to make sense of it. In other words, juxtaposition never tells us "the truth" but instead prompts us to discover the truth for ourselves.

Film didn't always work this way. In the beginning, there were no cuts. In the 1890s, when cinema was still in short trousers, films spooled out as single-take stories; a train arriving at a station, workers leaving a factory, a man playing the accordion and dancing. The End. So film started life as a recording medium only. The advent of editing turned film into a storytelling medium. Walter Murch, taking his cue from the Wright Brothers' first successful flight in an airplane, says, "Editing is what allowed films to take flight."

In the mid-teens of the last century, the first to fully explore the storytelling grammar of the cut was the pioneer filmmaker D.W. Griffith (*Birth of a Nation, Intolerance*). He did this of course by trial and error. "What if I jumped from this wide to a close-up right here — too shocking, too weird? Hey look at this, I just jumped from over there to over here. How does that make you feel? Like your head's going to explode?" It would be fascinating to know how he made his breakthroughs. We don't know because he didn't leave us many notes.

On the other hand, the early Soviet filmmakers, who were great admirers of Griffith, wrote a storm. They too experimented, and they declaimed, and argued and shook their fists. They were in a kind of fever about film; this new medium had just shown up and it seemed a perfect fit for their brave new world. At a time when the vast majority of the population was illiterate, they saw in film the possibility of telling big persuasive stories to the masses. And this was possible chiefly through the magic of juxtaposition.

The Kuleshov Effect

You maybe already know about this editing phenomenon, but let's do it again. Lev Kuleshov, a teacher and theorist at the world's first film school in Moscow, set up an experiment with his students to explore the expressive potential of the cut. Using a Medium Close Up shot (MCU) of a man looking straight ahead, he chose to cut

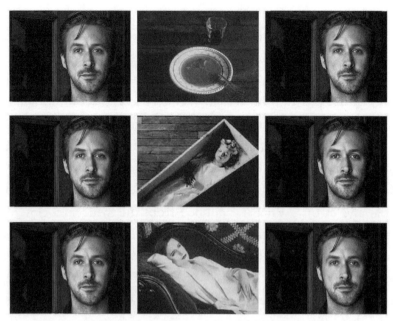

I found this version of the Kuleshov Effect with Ryan Gosling online — it's perfect.

this same shot with three different Point of View (POV) images: a bowl of soup, a child in a coffin, and a young woman.

So reading left to right, we see an uninflected shot of Ryan staring, then we see what he's looking at, and then we return to Ryan, and now this same image is inflected with a sense of hunger, then grief, then desire.

This famous experiment (which became known as the Kuleshov Effect) proved that no single image has an absolute meaning; shots change their meaning through juxtaposition with the next shot.

This effect is not unique to editing. Director Sergei Eisenstein (*Battleship Potemkin*), found examples of this juxtapositional effect in haiku poetry. He also demonstrates how it works in Chinese characters: Here one pictogram is combined with another to form a meaning:

"A dog + a mouth = 'to bark'; a mouth + a child = 'to scream'; a mouth + a bird = 'to sing'; a knife + a heart = 'sorrow,' and so on. But this is — film editing!" (*The Film Sense*)

So this was the silent era. Of course, everything changed with the advent of the talkies, and storytelling was increasingly carried by dialogue and sound design. But juxtaposition, the collision of images, still remains cinema's most potent storytelling device.

How can we screenwriters replicate this juxtapositional effect in our writing?

Across twenty snowy mountains
The only moving thing
Was the eye of a blackbird

This is the first stanza of a poem by Wallace Stevens *Thirteen Ways of Looking at a Blackbird*, but we could easily be reading action lines from a screenplay. With great economy, a film sequence is immediately formed in the mind of the reader, including shot sizes, moment of cut, and even a sense of duration. And these "shots" possess a poetic charge through juxtaposition (vast / tiny, stillness / movement, white / black, cold / warm). This chimes with Eisenstein's haiku / editing connection.

I found more recent authority for this idea when I discovered an online interview between a poet and a movie editor.

And not just any film editor. Walter Murch is surely one of the most brilliant film editors in the last fifty years, and certainly the most fertile thinker about the craft. In an interview with the poet Joy Katz, Murch talks about the "secretly architectural" nature of both poetry and film editing. He points to the relationship between the length of a line of poetry and the duration of a film shot. He then goes on to discuss the juxtapositional qualities of both:

> "Why does a poet choose to end one line where he does, on a particular word, even though it may make no grammatical sense to do so? Perhaps because . . . he wants to draw subtle attention to the last word in the line and the first word in the next. Similarly, I will keep a shot on screen until it feels rhythmically and contextually "ripe" . . . I want to draw subtle (and sometimes not so subtle) attention to the final image of the outgoing shot, and compare it with the first image of the next." (*Parnassus, Poetry in Review*)

To be clear, Walter Murch was not addressing screenwriters here, but as soon as we see screenwriting as a kind of poetry, his words seem astonishingly apt. And the truth of this becomes clear when you take a closer look at any good screenplay; again and again, we see a free-verse quality that, in a "secretly architectural" way, embeds juxtapositional shapes in the writing.

Exercises

This is easy. Go to YouTube and watch *Cutting Edge: The Magic of Movie Editing*. Although it's a few years old now, and few directors shoot on celluloid anymore, it's one of the best documentaries ever made on editing. You'll be particularly interested in the section on Kuleshov. (You'll find it near the interview with Tarantino where he's saying, "Those crazy Russians started fucking around with images and creating different emotional effects.")

Now search on YouTube for a clip called *Hitchcock's Pure Cinema: The Kuleshov Effect*. Here's Hitchcock showing how it works; first, he smiles at a baby, and now he's leering at a babe . . .

CHAPTER 3

MAGIC

*George Méliès gives us some abracadabra in our very
first for-the-cut strategy: the substitution splice*

SLEIGHT OF HAND and magic have always been associated with film editing. In 1896, magician-filmmaker George Méliès made a short film called *The Vanishing Lady*. A magician walks on stage with his female assistant. She sits on a chair and he covers her in a cloth. With a flourish, he pulls away the cloth — she's gone! He waves his arms in the air and tries to summon her back. *Whaaa!* A human skeleton suddenly appears on the chair. He banishes the skeleton, waves his hands, tugs the cloth, and — *ta-da!* — his female assistant reappears. Phew.

This was one of the first examples of what became known as the "substitution splice." Méliès stumbled on this trick one day while filming street life in the Place de l'Opéra. His camera jammed. After a few moments, he got the camera rolling again. Later when he saw the effect of the jam on the projected image, he was amazed — "I suddenly saw the Madeleine-Bastille bus changed into a hearse, and men changed into women."

In these early years before cinemas were invented, Méliès showed his films at fairgrounds. Film-as-fairground-ride is a great image. A ride is engineered for fun, thrill, motion, and emotion. And that's the core business of screenwriting.

Substitution Splice

The substitution splice is Méliès' gift to screenwriters. And the best place to use it is the scene break.

In the standard screenplay format that we all use, the scene break doesn't appear to be any kind of event — we're simply starting a new scene. There's nothing here to remind us that the outgoing and incoming scenes are actually images / sounds that snap together in a fraction of a second. A scene break is nearly always a cut, and you can use it as a juxtapositional opportunity that speaks volumes.

Substitution splices come in all flavors — some will echo the movement in one shot with the movement in another. (A small boy draws his finger across his throat > cut > an identically framed adult completes the gesture.) An object in one location is matched with the same object in a new location (the beautiful tattoo that covers the skin on Tom's back > cut > tattoo now shown stretched and framed in an art gallery). And then there are substitutions that use a proxy: Martha has a fever in one shot, and black mourning dresses hang on a clothesline in the next shot. Unexpected substitutions create surprise — a skeleton appears instead of the lady!

A huge number of substitutions center on a simple magician's device: The assistant steps into a hinged box, the door closes, and reopens to reveal . . .

```
The hero escapes the gang, jumps in the lift,
the door closes — cut — a gangster waits on
the ground floor and when the lift door opens —
it's empty!
```

A version of this last trick is memorably used in one of the big set pieces in *Silence of the Lambs*. Armed feds head towards the home of the serial killer "Buffalo Bill." Through parallel action, we see Bill's sadistic activities indoors, while the feds are surrounding the house. An undercover fed carries a bouquet of flowers to Bill's front door. He rings the bell. Bill opens it and — eh? Our hero Clarice Starling is standing there! Before we can gather our thoughts, we cut to the feds kicking down the front door of an empty house. And now we get it — the feds got the wrong address, and Clarice has unwittingly stumbled into the serial killer's lair.

So this is a substitution splice. Sometimes called "match cut" editing.

Maybe this sort of trick can appear a bit cheesy. In a sense, it is. Méliès said, "I must say, to my great regret, the cheapest tricks have the greatest impact." But properly judged, it can be the moment of epiphany in your story. Here's one you'll remember: a prehistoric hominid just discovers an animal bone makes a great weapon and slaughters his enemy. Then he throws it triumphantly in the air — cut — a bone-like spaceship floats in space. *2001 Space Odyssey*.

There's another classic substitution splice in *Lawrence of Arabia*. This is a "match cut" in both senses. It looks like this: World War I, and T.E. Lawrence has been summoned to the Arab Bureau in London for a briefing before he sets off to find Prince Faisal in Arabia. Bureau Chief Dryden is holding an unlit cigarette — Lawrence lights it for him. Then:

```
Lawrence contemplates the lighted match.
He blows it out.


Cut (Substitution splice)


Dawn. A desert horizon.
The sun mounts an Arabian sky.
```

This is my own "haiku" version of the script. In 1962, when this film was made, the editing convention for bridging scenes taking place in different locations, and different times, was a dissolve. That's just what we did back then: here we are in London > dissolve > Arabia desert. But editor Anne Coates and director David Lean watched a rough cut of the film before the labs had yet inserted the dissolve, and they were blown away by the straight cut.

This kind of substitution cut (flame / sun) triggers poetic associations in the viewer's imagination, and the viewer's imagination is greater, more powerful than anything we can hope to directly put on screen.

The play of poetic juxtapositions can be found in this extract from the screenplay *Beasts of the Southern Wild*:

```
EXT. MARINA PAUPIER NET — NIGHT
Wink opens his trawl net and dumps a massive
catch into a picking pan. There's food to feed
a hundred in the haul. No one is a bit fazed
though, this is just your average night fishing
in the Bathtub.

Shrimp, crabs, and small leaping fish struggle
over one another for dear life . . .

Hushpuppy focuses in on a tiny fish, wriggling
and sucking its last breaths of air.

             HUSHPUPPY (V.O.)
     One day, the storm's gonna blow, the
     ground's gonna sink, and the water's
     gonna rise up so high, there ain't gonna
```

```
be no Bathtub, just a whole bunch of
water.

She picks up a crab, pets its belly. The DIN
of the party fades down around her as she lis-
tens to its HEARTBEAT.

EXT. LADY JO'S CYPRESS FOREST — NIGHT
Explosions everywhere as Bathtubbers rampage
blasting fireworks down the street instead
of into the air. Men dressed as women, women
dressed as men, in some kind of reckless eso-
teric ritual.
```

So at the scene break we have a substitution of opposites: a child listening to the heartbeat of a crab > cut > explosions, fireworks, and a community in full fiesta.

But we can also detect the poetry of the cut in the collision of movement and stillness, life and death, the seething catch and the heartbeat of a single crab, the din of the crowd and the thoughts of a child, night and fiery light, and men dressed as women and women dressed as men.

Exercises

1. Revisit your own screen story, but this time in the company of Méliès. At each scene break, think about opportunities for some substitution magic. As the man says, don't worry if it seems cheap, as long as it's wow.

2. Go to YouTube and use the search terms "*Silence of the Lambs parallel editing*" to find the clip we discussed earlier. Write a short sequence of scenes, with minimal or no dialogue, that will deliver a similar shocking substitution.

CHAPTER 4

THREE AXES

*Suggestion, puzzle, and kinesis — three kinds of juxtaposition
that can turn a passive viewer into a story partner*

THE SUBSTITUTION SPLICE is just the start. In the next three chapters, we'll look in more detail at the narrative energy that can be released when you collide images, and how writers can capture this in the screenplay.

I quoted Stanton's "two plus two" formula earlier. The interesting thing about juxtaposition is that it sometimes prompts "four," but not always. In Hitchcock's demonstration of the Kuleshov Effect, when we watch both sequences (the baby and the babe), we can readily supply the thought "dear old uncle" and "dirty old man." But the *Beasts of the Southern Wild* substitution splice is clearly a different category of juxtaposition; there's no easy connection, and the audience is prompted to supply a more poetic, perhaps ineffable solution.

The purpose of *writing for the cut* is to draw the audience into discovering the story for themselves. Knowing how to write our cuts so that an intended story idea flowers in the imagination of the viewer is clearly a desirable thing. But how do you do that, and can you really have any control over the thoughts that spark in the viewer's mind?

This is a complex and probably quite subjective phenomenon

and, like poetry itself, may never be entirely mapped out. But I made a start. I spent a few years examining the construction of films and reading screenplays. I talked to feature film editors, and I read the literature around screenwriting and editing. A pattern emerged.

It seems to me there were three kinds of poetic juxtaposition, and each can trigger a different contribution from the viewer:

1. **Suggestion:** The cut ignites aesthetic and lyrical possibilities. The viewer adds *imagination* and *subtext*.

> Two girls with blood on their hands and face are running and screaming along a bushy track > cut > the same two girls are screaming with delight as they run towards their parents aboard an ocean liner. (*Heavenly Creatures*)

2. **Puzzle:** The cut creates mystery and piques curiosity. The viewer adds a *solution*.

> We're in Jackie's front room and a journalist is quietly asking her what the bullet sounded like > cut > We see two motorcycles speed up to the President's limousine as it races to hospital. (*Jackie*)

3. **Kinesis:** The cut creates a sense of motion, time, pattern, and rhythm. The viewer adds *emotion*.

> Renton kicks a ball against an urban brick wall > cut > a train pulls away to reveal Renton with two other figures standing in a big Scottish wilderness. (*T2 Trainspotting*)

Kinesis is the property of editing closest to music. It determines the intensity, tempo, and pitch of suggestion and puzzle. Kinesis is in fact everywhere present in the film from the rhythm of shot-reverse-shot dialogue, to the pacing of suspense and action-thriller sequences. It is the motor of the fairground ride.

So we have suggestion, puzzle, and kinesis. Of course, all scene breaks are necessarily juxtapositions, although in reality many carry minimal narrative freight: we're in the park > cut > now we're at the wedding reception. The cut says we've changed locations. Or think of a dialogue scene that very often will end up as a shot-reverse-shot sequence: he's talking, now she's talking, now he's talking again. The cut might be saying little more than "these guys are talking to each other in the same room." (There might be reaction shots here that speak volumes, but we'll come to that later.) Clearly there's sometimes more and sometimes less story-telling at the cut.

Now if we add this to the mix, then our diagram starts to look more like an XYZ graph, where each kind of juxtaposition has a sliding scale of intensity:

Suggestion > Statement
Puzzle > Exposition
Kinesis > Stasis

The cut can register on any and all of these axes at once. So the example I gave from *Heavenly Creatures* scores high on the suggestion axis, but it also presents a puzzle, and it's in motion.

Anything that sits at the far end of the scale (statement, exposition, stasis) is going to be pretty uninvolving. This might be a scene at a table in an Italian restaurant, and the hero is sharing his thoughts with two rival mobsters —

MICHAEL
My father couldn't make it here today on

```
account of you shot him a few times and
he's very ill. I asked you here so we can
talk — sort this out. You guys threaten
my family — move in on our business. This
is very troubling. (Pause) OK, I need to
go to the bathroom. I've hidden a gun
there, and when I come back I'm going
to shoot you in the head as revenge for
crossing my family.


MICHAEL returns from the bathroom and shoots
the mobsters dead.
```

So Michael is sharing his thoughts, which means there's no subtext, and he's telling us the plot so there's no puzzle. And when he returns from the bathroom and shoots the mobsters, it's a damp squib. There's nothing here for the audience to do, they're wondering if artichokes are in season.

How does it look if the cut tells the story? It looks like *The Godfather.*

So we're at the other end of the scale — suggestion, puzzle, kinesis — and the audience has to play catch-up: Michael Corleone heads to the toilet reaches behind the cistern and retrieves a gun. He returns to the table and Sollozzo is talking to him in Italian, but there are no subtitles. And Michael is just listening — not saying a word. We hear the metal-on-metal screech of a train somewhere nearby. Michael has a really troubled look on his face — Sollozzo still talking Italian. The screeching is so loud now, the train must be in the room. Michael stands and shoots Sollozzo and McCluskey in the head.

Now the cuts are inviting the audience to discover the story for themselves (What are these guys saying? What is Michael thinking?), feel the mounting suspense (While the screeching train sets our teeth on edge, we're thinking, "Will he go through with it? He's going to do it, no . . . yes . . . no . . . now!"), and experience terror and shock. (He shot him in the head!)

Of course, for most scenes in most films, much of the storytelling is not at the cut, but in the shot itself — it's right there in the dialogue, the action, the look, the mise-en-scene, and the cinematography. Nevertheless, the cut is the key mechanism for prompting the viewers' contribution to the story. And in a blink: "We're in another part of town," or "It's ten years later," or "She doesn't really love him;" or it might be other wordless revelations like "*He* hid the evidence," or "They're *sisters*," or "She's *protecting* him."

When we begin a new screenplay, or review work-in-progress, we can make it a habit to consider how much we're letting the cut tell the story.

In the broadest sense, this juxtapositional (Kuleshov) effect is quite simply the life pulse of all drama. John Yorke, who served as head of drama at both Channel 4 and the BBC, traces its origins right back to Greek tragedy, and writes:

> "Kuleshov stumbled on something far more than a clever editing technique: he discovered, though never fully appreciated, this simple, basic building block. Everything that follows — character, dialogue, multi-protagonism, thematic stranding, television structure — all of it flows from here. When two opposites are juxtaposed correctly, an explosion occurs, and the story comes alive." (*Into the Woods*)

The next three chapters will examine these poetic juxtapositions in more detail, and we'll see how they translate as writing strategies.

Exercises

When you juxtapose this action line with the next, you have the potential to hook the viewer through metaphor, paradox, alliteration, synecdoche, comparison, and contradiction. And while this might sound a little hifalutin, in practice this is rather like fooling around with fridge magnetic poetry.

There is in fact a really close kinship between *writing for the cut* and magnetic poetry. Musician-composer Dave Kapell devised this simple writing aid to overcome lyric block. It works a lot like editing. The obvious difference is that, as a screenwriter, you're creating your own stock of "images," and these are action lines, rather than single words.

1. Check magnetpoetry.com and hit the "play online" button. Enter a world of instant wonder.

2. Go to YouTube and enter search terms "*Godfather, Michael shoots Sollozzo.*" Watch it two or three times.

Now write this scene from memory as though it were a kind of fridge magnet poem. In other words, write in short lines, and in fragments — capture the jig of the cut.

CHAPTER 5

SUGGESTION

Suggestion is a lyrical kind of juxtaposition that invites the audience to add imagination and subtext

For-the-cut strategies:
- **SPLIT SCENE BREAK** — spill across the cut
- **NONLINEAR SHUFFLE** — move the parts around

Sometimes when I catch a flight, I like to watch movies without a headset and allow the imagery alone to tell the story. The poetry of suggestion is how silent films told their stories; they used symbol, gesture, action, and the cut to trigger the imagination of the viewer. There were captions too, but for the most part this really was the era of "show, don't tell." This spirit has never gone away.

Alexander Mackendrick, film director and seminal teacher at CalArts, said this about the nature of film:

"Though (cinema) can produce reams of dialogue, it can also tell stories purely in movement, in action and re-action . . . Cinema delivers such an inordinate quantity of data that the verbal component becomes secondary to the image. Consequently the essential and underlying meaning of film is often much more effectively transmitted by a complex and intricate organization of cinematic elements that are not only not verbal, but can never be fully analyzed by verbal means." (*On Film-Making*)

The advent of sound in the 1920s was a boon, of course. But in the beginning, it fostered a special brand of naturalism, and storytelling shifted its center of gravity towards dialogue. Editing too became more prosaic and signaled its intentions like this:

1. The hero runs up the steps > cut > opens the front door (these two places are close together).

2. The hero catches a village bus > dissolve > jumps off in the city (these two places are far apart, and time has passed).

3. The hero is looking pensive > ripple dissolve > a small child is playing on the beach (the hero is having a flash-back moment).

4. There's a terrific wind blasting through the hero's kitchen > dissolve > the wall calendar shows the months racing by (the hero is taking a long time recovering from that riding accident).

Then in the 1950s, the French New Wave showed up, and films got hip. Films like *The 400 Blows*, *Hiroshima Mon Amour*, and *Breathless* stripped out many of these editing conventions obliging the viewer to play catch-up: Is this new image sequential, later that day, in the past, or a dream? This wasn't just an editing revolution; the screenplays were experimenting with new ways to tell stories that sparkled with suggestion, puzzle, and kinesis. These arthouse films shook up the commercial movie industry too and influenced a new generation of American filmmakers. (Check out the American New Wave, a golden period of director-driven movies from around the mid-'60s to the early '80s — films like *Easy Rider*, *The Conversation*, *Bonnie and Clyde*, and *Five Easy Pieces*.)

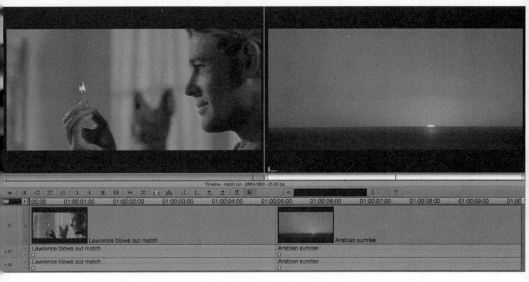

Top left is the Source Window — this is where you select material from your rushes.
Top right is the Program Window — this is where you preview your cut.
Lower third of the screen is devoted to the timeline — this is where you assemble your film.
In this timeline, you can see video (V1) and two audio channels (A1 and A2). There are two
clips here with a vertical cut in the middle.

More on this later. First, I want to talk about the editing inter-
face and connect the screenplay directly to the cut.

So the scene break we described in *Lawrence of Arabia* is what
an editor calls a "straight cut" (also called a hard or butt cut) —
meaning the video and the audio cut together at the same moment.

We're now going to look at another common cut — the split
edit, and then discuss the screenwriting equivalent.

The split edit (also called a "L" or "J" cut) is a staggered cut
where the audio of the outgoing shot continues under the visuals
of the incoming shot (or the other way around)

It looks like this:

In this timeline, you can see the cut is now staggered, with audio continuing under the
incoming images.

Split scene break

The screenwriting equivalence of a split edit we might term a "split scene break." John Truby, author of a seminal screenwriting manual called *The Anatomy of Story*, gives an example of this editing shape being used as far back as 1931 in the screenplay for the Fritz Lang film *M*:

> "In *M*, a child murderer buys a little girl a balloon. In the next scene, a woman prepares dinner and then calls for her child, Elsie. As she continues to call the little girl's name, the visual track splits from the soundtrack, and the audience sees an empty stairwell, a block of apartments, Elsie's empty chair, and her plate and spoon at the kitchen table while the ever more desperate cries of the mother calling 'Elsie!' are heard. The visual line ends with the shot of a balloon that catches in some electrical wires and then floats away. This contrast between the sound line and the visual line produces one of the most heartbreaking moments in the history of film." (*The Anatomy of Story*)

It looks like this:

INT. APARTMENT — DAY The Mother leans over the communal stairwell and calls for her daughter.	

She enters the apartment, closes the door, and goes to the kitchen window — she calls again for her daughter.
 	
             MOTHER
  Elsie!

[The picture cuts here but the audio continues . . .]	
INT/EXT. APARTMENT BLOCK, VARIOUS LOCATIONS — DAY A drying room — washing hanging under the rafters MOTHER (V.O.) Elsie!	
Elsie's empty chair, and her plate and spoon at the kitchen table. MOTHER (V.O.) Elsie!	
A utility pole — Elsie's balloon is snagged in the overhead wires. MOTHER (V.O.) Elsie!	

It wasn't the editor who discovered this juxtaposition between word and image in the cutting room; it was written that way by Thea von Harbou. She was *writing for the cut*.

Used appropriately, this splitting technique can lift both the poetry and the forward motion of the story.

Here's a more recent example. I was interviewing Richard Hughes about cutting a horror film called *It Never Sleeps*, and he described a problem he was having. The scenes were written like this:

INT. DELI — DAY
The slack hour, the
café is almost empty.
Joan and Rachel are
chatting over a cup
of coffee at a corner
table.

*(Extract from much
longer dialogue
scene . . .)*

      RACHEL
How was it this
time?

      JOAN
It was . . . I
don't know — seems
like all we do is
talk — but I think
it's helping . . .

      RACHEL
Got to keep at
it, Joan — you
still doing
those breathing
exercises?

      JOAN
Yeah — it's all
good . . .

INT. JOAN'S
HOUSE, VARIOUS
LOCATIONS — DAY
Bare dining room —
Joan settles herself
at the table, drinks
a glass of water, and
listens to the sounds
of the house around
her.

Small kitchen — she takes the glass into the kitchen, then checks the window is locked.	
Patio door — she locks, opens, and then locks the patio door again to make sure.	
Front hall — she locks and bolts the front door.	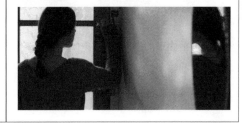

So the first scene is very talky and flying at a low altitude along the statement / exposition / stasis axes as Joan describes her PTSD therapy. The second scene shows her obsessive-compulsive routine.

To give this sequence a suggestive kick, the editor did the *M* trick: a split edit.

"By using the dialogue (of the two women in conversation) as voiceover into the next scene, we can introduce another level, a juxtaposition where what we're seeing now contradicts what Joan is saying. We're seeing the hero sitting alone in her room looking stressed, staring at a glass of water, and in voiceover, she's cheerfully saying the therapy's going well, she's feeling good. Now you open the whole thing up creatively in the sound world too. There's a tension here, the sequence is much more suggestive. And so the sound designers then took it to the next level."

So after he performed a split edit, the script/sequence looked like this:

```
INT. DELI — DAY
The slack hour, the café is almost empty. Joan
and Rachel are chatting over a cup of coffee at
a corner table.

Extract from much longer dialogue scene . . .)


                  RACHEL
      How was it this time?


                   JOAN
      It was . . . I don't know — seems like
      all we do is talk . . .


The conversation continues —

INT. JOAN'S HOUSE, VARIOUS LOCATIONS — DAY
Bare dining room — Joan settles herself at the
table, drinks a glass of water, and listens to
the sounds of the house around her.


                JOAN (V.O.)
      — but I think it's helping . . .


Small kitchen — she takes the glass into the
kitchen, then checks the window is locked.
```

```
                    RACHEL (V.O.)
        Got to keep at it, Joan — you still doing
        those breathing exercises?


    Patio door — she locks, opens, and then
    re-locks the patio door to make sure.


                    JOAN (V.O.)
        Yeah — it's all good . . .


    Front hall — she locks and bolts the front door.
```

And now we're making cinema.

Subtext

When the cut delivers a suggestive kick such as this, the audience might add subtext. Subtext is a very desirable thing in film storytelling. Director Mike Nichols (*The Graduate*) gives a neat definition:

> "I've always been impressed by the fact that upon entering a room full of people, you find them saying one thing, doing another, and wishing they were doing a third . . . The words are secondary and the secrets are primary. That's what interests me most." (*New York Times*)

Secrets, hidden desires, and true intentions can sometimes be expressed in more conventional ways such as voiceover. This is legitimate, of course, particularly if the writing is sharp and tangy like the "cool girl" monologue in *Gone Girl*. Exceptionally it might be expressed through dialogue: In *Amadeus,* Salieri's madness allows him the special privilege of soliloquizing his own subtext. Famously, in the film *Annie Hall*, subtext appeared as subtitles alongside the spoken word.

But juxtapositions — particularly reaction shots — are a far more common way to signal subtext.

<pre>
                         HANK
         Hey, Chloe. Can we have that bridal bouquet?
         I guess you won't be needing it now . . .

     (Cut) Chloe gives a brave smile.
</pre>

There is another effective for-the-cut technique that happens at the scene break; this one we will call "nonlinear shuffle."

Nonlinear shuffle

At one end of the scale, nonlinear shuffle means the shuffling of entire scenes to form new "wrongly" ordered configurations. At the other end, it might be the "intercutting" of two different scenes. Nonlinear shuffle was the term film editor-director Lisa Gunning used. She gives an example from the film *Nowhere Boy*, the film about John Lennon's early life growing up in Liverpool:

"There is a scene of the mother and John listening to Screamin' Jay Hawkins 'I Put A Spell On You' and they're listening together and the mother's painted nails brush against John's thigh. I made another montage there . . . I intercut this moment with a sex scene in the forest with this young girl who also happens to have the same red nail varnish . . ."

Now the audience can't help adding an Oedipal subtext. And where there was only a single break between two scenes, with Lisa's version there are several. This increases the number of juxtapositions, creates new rhythms and patterns, and has the potential to ramp up the poetic / subtextual power of a scene. This works a bit like parallel action (described later in the Kinesis section) — but whereas parallel action intercuts scenes occurring at the same time, nonlinear-shuffle intercuts scene fragments backwards and forwards in time in a way that may be uncanny, illogical, but entirely like the dream dimension of cinema.

For some reason, sex scenes are particularly suited to this kind of shuffling. Maybe this points to the difficulty of showing this most intimate act as a straight-in-your face scene. When a sex scene shows up in a drama, we can sometimes feel uncomfortably like voyeurs. Or it can sometimes seem mechanical — sex is too literally a playing out of secret desires, and we feel a lack of complexity, or mystery.

Editor Anne Coates describes using a nonlinear shuffle in the film Out of Sight. In a seduction scene that takes place in a hotel restaurant, she shuffles the lovers' flirtatious conversation with fragments of the adjacent sex scene. The resulting sequence interweaves flirtation, foreplay, and sex in a manner that is enigmatic, erotic, amusing, and quite dreamlike.

There is a strong kinship here between this shuffle shape and anastrophe, which works something like Natalie Dorsch's arresting poem:

I walked up the door,
Shut the stairs,
Said my shoes,

Took off my prayers,
Turned off my bed,
Got into the light,
All because,
You kissed me goodnight.

Perhaps one of the most famous sex scene shuffles is in *Don't Look Now*. In the original version, the film censors found the scene too graphic and insisted on cuts. Director Nicholas Roeg's solution was to intercut the scene with the adjacent post-coital scene. By juxtaposing intense images of two people sexually united, with images of the same couple, quietly and separately getting dressed for dinner, the sequence seems to reveal something profound about the human condition.

In an interview some years later, Roeg said, "A lot of filmmaking can be linked to prestidigitation, you know — a shuffling of the cards." (*film4productions.com*)

I borrowed this technique for a different kind of scene in my own screenplay *Rush the Sky*. This is a thriller that tells the story of two teenage, adrenaline-addicted lovers, Luke and Ella. The opening scenes shows Luke taking a shower in a highly distressed state — only later in the story does the audience come to understand that Luke has just witnessed the gangland murder of a young boy. Here is an early draft of the scene:

```
INT. VALERIE'S FLAT, BATHROOM — NIGHT
Luke is out of breath. He stares at his own
frightened face in the mirror. There's blood
on his cheek.


He snaps off the light.
```

Faint moonlight. In the shower, Luke is vigor-
ously scrubbing his body.

He's seized by a violent fit of shaking. He
slumps to his knees.

So, after my conversation with Lisa, I shuffled a section of dialogue from a scene that plays much later in the script, and now it
looks like this:

INT. VALERIE'S FLAT, BATHROOM — NIGHT
Luke is out of breath. He stares at his own
frightened face in the mirror. There's blood
on his cheek.

He snaps off the light.

                    VALERIE (V.O.)
     Here comes the storm. And the sky is like
     an ocean. It covers the sun.
     "Help, help, where's the ark?"

Faint moonlight. In the shower, Luke is vigor-
ously scrubbing his body.

                    VALERIE (V.O.)
     But there is no ark, not this time.
     And it rains like the ocean is falling.

He's seized by a violent fit of shaking — he
slumps to his knees.

The viewer can't know at this point that this is his mother's voice and is taken from a flashback scene when Luke was a child. The scene now invites the viewer to make a poetry / puzzle connection between Luke cleansing himself of "sin," and the coming of a great storm of retribution. And there is an added bonus — later when Valerie's scene plays out in its proper place, the audience will recall the words, and it may well strike them as a "prophecy foretold."

This principle can be taken to the next level where shuffling whole scenes to new locations can create surprising neighbors, and increases the possibility of serendipitous "ignitions" (on all three axes). Many screenwriters are familiar with this strategy; for example: Christopher Nolan's screenplay *Memento*, Guillermo Arriaga's *21 Grams*, Simon Beaufoy's *Slumdog Millionaire*), and Noah Oppenheim's *Jackie*. This shuffling is far from random; in all cases, the structure reveals a complex narrative logic. Screenwriter Arriaga describes how he began experimenting:

"I started putting different scenes together with no time connection between one and the other. I jumped from one scene in the present to one in the past to one in the future to one in the past, and so on . . . We all know that one scene has a meaning by itself and a completely different one when it is linked to a scene before and a scene after . . . I was looking for a way to make the audience be much more participative — to have a constant dialogue with the film, to create and recreate the story." (*Script*)

Below are some suggested exercises. Like others later in this book, these ones are "rapid prototyping" ideas for developing your story. Work rapidly like a film editor: "Let's try this. Doesn't work? Let's try this. Doesn't work? Let's try this. Hmmm . . . better."

Exercises

1. Screenwriters can learn much about how to simulate in words the dynamics of the cut by reading haiku poetry. If you're new to haiku, Google some examples online; you'll get the idea in no time. Now write some action lines for your screenplay in the style of a haiku poem. Don't get snagged on the form; you're not really writing haiku — you're writing the beats of your story in a compressed form and looking to create juxtapositions. Maybe we should call this a new kind of beat poetry.

2. Write two short scenes with the intention of creating a split scene break that suggests subtext. Scene 1 must have dialogue, and Scene 2 must be image / sound / action only. Now write two short scenes where the split works the other way around. Scene 1 is all image / sound / action, and this time the dialogue from the second scene invades the first scene in voiceover.

3. Using your own screen story, write a scene where juxtapositions within the action lines / dialogue suggest subtext.

4. Or write fresh scenes using these prompts:
   - He doesn't really love her.
   - She doesn't believe her mother's story.
   - He thinks his boss's idea will be a disaster.
   - She'd rather be talking to those cool cats over there.
   - She really wants to push a knife through his black heart.

CHAPTER 6

PUZZLE

*We can remove or reorder the jigsaw pieces to
draw the audience to find a solution*

For-the-cut strategies:
- **ELLIPSIS** — don't show, don't tell
- **IN MEDIAS RES** — start in the middle
- **SCRIPT-PLANNED MONTAGE** — poetry in motion
- **OPENING / TITLE SEQUENCE** — overture

In 1989, film editor Liao Ching-sung was editing *A City of Sadness*. After a few weeks, he'd show up for work, review his cut, and discover scenes had mysteriously gone missing. It seems the Director Hsiao-Hsien Hou was going into the suite at night and removing them. When Liao asked him why, Hou said he just didn't like those scenes anymore, they showed the audience too much. Liao tried to reason with him:

> "'Director, you can't do this. The scenes are not connecting. If we keep doing this, the movie will be a mess. It will be incomprehensible.' Knowing Hou was set on this strategy, I started to edit with the mindset of a Tang Dynasty poet, using the same kind of emotional, poetic logic to assemble the film. I realized that there were in fact many things the audience didn't need to know, things I could just get rid of . . ." (*FilmCraft: Editing*)

Just to remind ourselves what a Tang poem looks like, here's the first four lines of a verse that celebrates a great tidal bore that sweeps along the Qiantang River:

Thunder heard a hundred miles,
The song of the lute falls still.
Horsemen stream from the compound gate
And riverside watch for the tide.

The verse is a master class in economy: big visual / aural impact conveyed in the smallest number of words (in the context of film editing, let's just say Tang is doing something similar to haiku — sorry to everyone in China and Japan). Each line is a fresh idea: thunder, lute, horsemen, riverside. "The scenes are not connecting," but this is precisely how the viewer is drawn to complete the story.

This chapter is about juxtapositions that create puzzle; and sometimes puzzle can be created simply by removing information "things the audience didn't need to know . . ."

Editing itself is often described as a puzzle. Back in the 1920s when Cecil B. De Mille's longtime editor Anne Bauchens was asked about her craft, she said:

"I would say it is very much like a jigsaw puzzle, except that in a jigsaw puzzle the little pieces are all cut out in the various forms and you try to fit them together to make a picture, while in cutting films you have to cut your pieces first and then put them together." (*We Make the Movies*)

She might also have added that there's no picture on the lid of the box, and that in any case the pieces are not predisposed to make any single picture. And one final difference: the audience completes the puzzle.

When we start to design a new screen story, we may often write in a linear way, and we're likely to include a great deal of exposition. And at this pre-script stage, it's probably essential — we're mapping the full journey of the story for ourselves. But later, when we've moved on to the treatment phase, we'll want to hide some of the map and allow the audience to find their own way.

So here's a short example of what it looks like when we don't hide the map.

INT. POLICE HQ: INCIDENT ROOM — DAY
Several Plainclothes are finishing a messy
working lunch. Detective Plensky suddenly
stands and tosses a crime file on the table.

                    PLAINCLOTHES 1
                     (Sarcastic)
        Hey — you got a lead?

                      PLENSKY
        Heading over to the docks.

                    PLAINCLOTHES 2
        How come?

                      PLENSKY
        Those Tattoo Brothers are gonna make
        their move — just found a clue in the
        report — maybe you missed something? Drug
        boat's coming in at three — no hurry,
        boys, finish your pickle.

```
She heads swiftly to the door.


INT. POLICE HQ: LOBBY — DAY
Det. Plensky exits the lift, walks across the
lobby, signs out at reception, and pushes
through the swing doors.


EXT. BUSY URBAN STREET — DAY
She strides across a busy sidewalk towards a
waiting unmarked car. Opens the door. Gets in,
puts on the seat belt. Turns on the radio —
pumping rock. She's gone.
```

In this scene we've been told what she's deduced, where she's going, who is making a move, and shown in near real time how she gets from the incident room to the car. This is what we might call chauffeur-driven storytelling — the driver is taking care of the entire journey, so the viewer can comfortably curl up in the back and fall asleep.

Now if you hide the map and go for Tang, it might look more like this:

```
INT. POLICE HQ: INCIDENT ROOM — DAY
Several Plainclothes are finishing a messy
working lunch.
Det. Plensky suddenly stands.
All eyes on Plensky —

                    PLENSKY
      It's now.


She throws a crime file on the table.
```

```
INT. POLICE CAR — DAY

Det. Plensky is driving fast through the
docklands.


                    PLENSKY
                  (on radio)
      Tattoo brothers . . . the youngest has a
      history of violence . . . no hurry, boys
      — grab some dessert.
```

In a single cut, the detective is in a speeding car, and the audience has to play catch-up to solve where she's heading, to whom she's talking, and what she's saying. There's also a kinetic substitution, as the cut now falls between the flying file and the moving car.

Of course, there will always be scenes where your characters have to spout backstory because it's simply not guessable, and the audience needs to know. And if this is the case then you need to find cunning ways to deliver exposition and keep the viewer busy. You could try Blake Snyder's famous "Pope in the Pool" strategy described in *Save the Cat!* It goes like this: some guys have come to Rome to let the Pope know about a plot to kill him. Oh, man, this is going to be a really dull, talky scene. But no, the scene actually plays out in the Vatican where the Pope is listening to the plot while doing laps in a pool. And so, as Blake puts it, the audience is thinking, "'I didn't know the Vatican had a *pool*?! And look, the Pope's not wearing his Pope clothes, he's . . . he's . . . in his bathing suit!' And before you can say, 'Where's my miter?' the scene's over."

Exposition is anathema to cinema. As a viewer, we know immediately when we're in the presence of this narrative stodge: action grinds to a halt, and dialogue becomes laden with backstory and plot detail. In editing terms, exposition is cutting together procedural continuity shots (the detective leaving the room, exiting the elevator, etc.), or it is the joining of "literal" shots:

```
            MOM (pointing excitedly)
      Look, Melissa — here comes the party
      clown!


(Cut) A party clown appears at the door.
```

When we look back at movies from earlier times, this kind of signaling was common. But screen storytelling moves on, and the way we write and cut film stories should be at the frontier of the audience's visual-aural literacy.

```
                  BETTY
      Do you get this movie?


                   BOB
      Of course I get it.


                  BETTY
      You think it's operating at the frontier
      of your visual-aural literacy?


                   BOB
      Stop bugging me.
```

Many viewers would probably find it totally alien to have to explain how they've solved the clues the screenwriter has sewn into the story; much of this kind of inductive processing goes on at a subliminal level. But we're constantly exercising this muscle:

we watch many more screen stories than our parents do, and way more than our grandparents did. TV and web grazing have made us all experts in the art of narrative infill. Bang! A gun goes off, a man is falling, a motorbike speeds over a bridge, a woman is weeping, an ocean of wheat ripples in the wind . . . we identify the genre, pick up the clues, and join the dots.

Story is how we make sense of the world; if there's no evident story, we look for a pattern and supply a story of our own. *Writing for the cut* plays to this essential human trait.

Ellipsis: don't show, don't tell

With this in mind, one strategy for *writing for the cut* is to deliberately make gaps: don't show, don't tell. Taking our cue from *A City of Sadness*, one can reduce exposition and increase puzzle by simply removing scenes and dialogue, and breaking the thread. As editor-director Lisa Gunning says:

> "Gaps in the story can be strangely effective. If the audience engages emotionally with the character then the gaps are easy to fill. Filling in the gaps in a story is fun. Encouraging an audience to do this creates a sense of additionality. Their imagination is far better than anything that you can put on a screen."(Interview with Lisa Gunning)

This can be a risky strategy of course; if the gap is well judged, the viewer will generate the narrative electricity to arc the gap. If too wide, then there may be no spark, and the viewer is left confused and heading for the exit.

In the early '70s, Walter Murch was working on a five-hour cut of Coppola's *The Conversation*, trying to edit it down to a reasonable commercial length.

"— I would have the feeling that I couldn't remove a certain scene, because it so clearly expressed what we were after. But after hesitating, I'd cut it anyway . . . forced to because of the length of the film. Then I'd have this paradoxical feeling that by taking away something I now had even more of it. It was almost biblical in its idea of abundance. How can you take away something and wind up with more of it?" (*The Conversations*)

Murch saw that some key scenes, ones that seemed to "shine" the theme of the film very brightly, could cast into shadow those scenes where the theme was more subtly stated. He has a good thumbnail for this: "You pay attention to the stars on nights when there is no moon."

At the most extreme end of the gap strategy is "the missing reel." For their grindhouse film *Planet Terror*, directors Robert Rodriguez and Quentin Tarantino deliberately removed a reel (that's twenty minutes of screen time by the way) from the second act of the film, and replaced it with a caption reading "missing reel." When the story recommenced in the third act, audiences had to intuit the missing plot based on the new coordinates.

David Mamet is also a fan of this strategy; he suggests the best way to improve any film is to burn the first reel. Now if you burned the first reel, you'd have a story that started in the middle of things. And that might be a brilliant place to start.

Start in the middle of things

In the cutting room a question that exercises editors as they start on a new film is: "Where does the story begin?" Screenwriters may find this surprising — they've labored long and hard on their opening scenes, why would it change? But in the edit suite, kinetic and narrative imperatives bear down on the cut nowhere more keenly than the opening scenes. We can never know what percentage of opening scenes get "rewritten" in the edit suite, but it could be as much as 50%.

Lisa Gunning edited Anthony Minghella's film *Breaking and Entering*. When she read the script and viewed the rushes,

> "— it occurred to me the first 35 scenes were all about setting the characters up . . . But for me the film started the moment there was a break-in (*which happens somewhere around page 20 — that's the length of a reel!*). You don't want to start off with an explanation, you want to start with something that's intriguing, something that makes you think, 'What is this?' You want the audience to feel curious . . . I enjoy films that start *in medias res*; you feel like you're in the middle of something and you have to find your way out of that. So I said to Anthony, 'Could we just try cutting out the first 35 scenes?'"

Minghella's script had a really long set-up, so the editor entirely reconfigured the scenes in a way that was for the cut, and began the story at the moment of significant action: the break-in.

But Lisa didn't throw all those earlier scenes away, instead she sliced and diced and made an opening montage.

Montage

In many parts of the world, "montage" simply means editing. In English-speaking countries, it refers to a particular editing figure — often a short, rapidly cut sequence of images accompanied by music. The purpose of a montage is usually to condense time, or to conjure up an era, a place, a relationship, a community, or a backstory.

For many, seeing the word "montage" in a script is a kind of violation — it's a production word — so don't use it 'less you lookin' get yerself killed.

Manual maven Robert McKee has a different objection:

> "Like the Dream Sequence, the montage is an effort to make undramatized exposition less boring by keeping the audience's eye busy. With few exceptions, montages are a lazy attempt to substitute decorative photography and editing for dramatization and are, therefore, to be avoided." (*Story*)

Clearly "keeping the audience's eye busy" is a fairly vacuous substitution for dramatized exposition. But this partly misses the point — the best montages appeal to the eye for sure, but their primary purpose is to appeal to the emotions. And while the emotions are engaged, a montage can smuggle in a slice of story by setting the viewer a puzzle. If this is done well, then this is what Hitchcock would call "pure cinema." Done badly, and you have a series of musical postcards.

When you see a montage in a feature film, it may have been written that way. But just as likely the editor created it to fix a problem. For example, a cluster of expositional scenes were slowing the film down, so the editor suggests: "Let's travel light and allow the audience to discover the story."

Lisa is cutting *Nowhere Boy* and —

> "— the way the story was written, there's a long section about this guitar thing. He'd been given a guitar by his Aunt Mimi and it was his favorite possession and he misses school and behaves badly so Mimi confiscates his guitar and then there's a process of him going to his biological mother, borrowing the money from her and buying the guitar back and telling Mimi to fuck off. And this is all about the triangular interplay between the three characters: John and his two mothers. But in editing, when watched

chronologically, it just went on and on. She's angry and that thread of the story just lent itself to montage, because then you see this happen and you see that happen and he gets his guitar back. And using the music from the first Beatles concert he plays in, using the guitar music from that concert as a sound-bed for those scenes, and ending at the concert, seemed like a good solution. That's around 15 pages of script condensed into a montage that's two minutes long."

This is intelligent montage. At its best, montage can be the purest most poetic form of cinema — it can "show" story by using a cinematic shorthand. When professional screenwriters write this kind of montage, they tend to break it down into scenes, and each scene might contain an important beat. There would be puzzle and poetry at the scene break. And there may be snatches of dialogue too. They rarely upset anyone by actually writing the word "montage."

Film director Karel Reisz calls this kind of construction "script-planned montage."

Script-planned montage

In his book *Technique of Film Editing*, Reisz describes a sequence in *Citizen Kane* that shows the gradual and painful break-up of Kane and Susan's marriage over time. This variety of montage again deploys music, but uses an elliptical, patterned, and juxtapositional style of construction. And it uses dialogue and synchronous sound. And that is exactly how it was written in the script.

Here's another example of a script-planned montage from a more recent film. Towards the end of *Slumdog Millionaire*, our young hero-from-the-slums Amir has reached the finals of the quiz show *Who Wants to Be a Millionaire?* Now fortune hangs on one final question:

```
INT. STUDIO. NIGHT
. . . the lights dim, the music rumbles. Prem
(quiz show host) pushes the button on his com-
puter. Gets conversational.

                    PREM
        Big reader, are you Amir? A lover of
        literature?

Amir just shrugs.

                    AMIR
        I can read.

Nervous laughter from the audience.

                    PREM
        Lucky! In Alexander Dumas' book, The
        Three Musketeers, two of the musketeers
        are called Athos and Porthos. What was
        the name of the third musketeer? Was it
        A) Aramis, B) Cardinal Richelieu, C)
        D'Artagnan, D) Planchet.

An involuntary laugh comes out of Amir's
mouth.
```

INT. SCHOOL. DAY.

A flash of Mister Nandha the schoolteacher
crashing the book down on Amir's head.

INT. SCHOOL. DAY.

Rows of children reading.

                    MISTER NANDHA

        Next chapter on Monday when Athos and
        Porthos meet the third musketeer.

EXT. SLUM. DAY.

Another flash of Mister Nandha among the riot-
ers running up the street towards them, hate
on his face, knife in hand.

EXT. BUILDER'S YARD. NIGHT

Monsoon rain. Amir and Salim, huddled in their
concrete pipes.

                        AMIR

        She can be the third musketeer.

EXT. ORPHANAGE. PATH. NIGHT.

The teenage Amir is humming along cheerfully
to his song as they walk down the path towards
the shack where he is to be blinded.

                        SALIM

                (conversationally)

        Athos.

Amir is suddenly alert. Slows

                    AMIR
        Porthos?

Salim nods. Big smile. Puts his hand on Amir's
shoulder.

                    SALIM
        When I say.

                    PUNNOOSE
                (glancing back)
        Come on.

INT. ROADSIDE SHACK. NIGHT
In the shack, sitting on an upturned oil drum,
surrounded by puzzled Indians in rags, a slow
smile comes to Latika's face.

EXT. STUDIO. BACKSTAGE. NIGHT.
The Inspector and Sergeant Srinivas get out
of the police car and run to the backstage
door. The inspector opens it and stands, file
in hand, watching Amir on stage through a gap
in the set.

INT. STUDIO. NIGHT
Camera on Prem

                    PREM
      The million-rupee question: and he's
      smiling. I guess you know the answer.

                    AMIR
      Would you believe it? I don't.

This is montage: It mimics the agility of the mind under pressure to process a great many thoughts very quickly. And it is also "dramatized exposition." Simon Beaufoy is *writing for the cut.*

Title / Opening Sequence

Another species of montage can be found at the very start of a film. Filmmakers are often contractually bound to include titles at the start of a film; this may be packaged in a specially designed title sequence. Or the titles may be superimposed or interwoven amongst the opening shots of the film. Some writers structure their script to accommodate titles, but it's not common practice. Maybe it should be.

The convention of titles at the start of a movie is interesting because it tends to fragment the opening, and this in turn gestures towards a montage / overture approach. Here's Lisa Gunning again:

"Once you see 'produced by', 'directed by' that gives you license for fragmentation . . . I'd say the title sequence was an opportunity at the script stage to really think about how you can use that language of fragmentation . . . An awful lot of the time the script totally ignores the presence of any titles. If you're lucky it'll say 'credits' and move on quickly. And that's a wasted opportunity . .

. you could be showing very simple images in vignette form and then intercut with captions. That gives you this sentence structure that's very different, it's like bullet points . . ."

At the London Screenwriters' Festival in 2013, the film editor Chris Dickens gave a master class at an event called "Your Script in the Cutting Room." He showed the opening sequence of *Slumdog Millionaire* as it was originally written and cut. He explained that at test screenings audiences found it raised false expectations about the film. Then he showed the nonlinear recut version that now opens the film.

"Those scenes — overlapping dialogue, making it nonlinear, out of real time — was actually like the structure of the film itself. Essentially it was preparing you for this experience . . . once you've set that up and the audience is prepared for it, you can go anywhere."

Exercises

1. Save a new copy of your screenplay and sharpen your knife. Look for a run of scenes that convey a slice of exposition in an orderly, logical way. Now remove all or part of it to create a brutal gap. Now read from a scene or two back and check the new outgoing / incoming images — is there good juju here or does it go *phut*? Work it some more — you really want to break your screenplay into fragments and move the parts around — that's where the new comes from.

2. Open your screenplay and cut the first 20 pages (or how-ever many it takes before you get to significant action). Now create an opening / title sequence using some of those scenes from the first 20 pages. Do it quickly. Reconfigure. Do it again.

3. In your screenplay look for a moment in the story where there is some kind of change over time (a relationship, a stakeout, jack-to-a-king, etc.). Rewrite as a script-planned montage.

CHAPTER 7

KINESIS . . .

Slicing and dicing time to put movement into our story —
the cut creates motion, and the audience adds emotion

For-the-cut strategies:
- **PARALLEL ACTION** — the thrill of cross-cutting
- **ACTION SCENES** — writing the set piece
- **SUSPENSE** — stretching those nerves
- **DIALOGUE** — another kind of action

On the film *Jaws* director Stephen Spielberg often clashed with his editor Verna Fields over the exact moment to cut on almost every scene involving the animatronic shark. Spielberg always wanted to hold the shot longer . . .

"— but the sad fact was that the shark would only look real in 36 frames and not 38 frames. And that 2 frame difference was the difference between something really scary, and something that looked like a great white floating turd." (*The Magic of Movie Editing*)

Two frames is a tiny fraction of a second, but long enough to make a big difference. Editing is a highly nuanced craft where the decision to cut or not to cut is guided by the experience, film memory, and aesthetic predilections of the editor.

The telling of film stories is by definition kinetic. Editors "make" kinesis in the slicing and dicing of time, the forward momentum of the story, and the rhythmic patterning of sequences. It is both motion and emotion.

How can screenwriters convey any of this?

There's very little in the screenwriter's creative world that hints at the time and rhythm imperatives of film beyond the familiar "one page equals one minute of screen time."

So, back to poetry. Our bridge to kinesis is the rhythmic pulse of poetry — pithy dialogue, laconic present-tense action lines, parallel action, use of em-dash, exclamation, "beat," and a whole constellation of other time cues. This scene goes rat-ta-tat-tat, and this one goes *Shall I compare thee to a summer's day?*

Parallel Action

Kinesis is the force that animates all film genres, but as a viewer, we feel it most keenly in suspense and action-thrillers. Parallel action is one of our favorite rides.

Parallel action is a pattern that writers have known about since we first started cutting film (Eisenstein finds parallel action in the pre-cinema literature of Charles Dickens). The thrill of parallel action derives from the rapid zigzag motion of the story. It usually plays out as a sequence of crosscuts between scenes occurring simultaneously in different locations, which often converge into one.

One of the earliest examples is the 1907 short film *The Fatal Hour*, written and directed by the first "master of suspense," D.W. Griffith. Here we see a masked fiend tie and gag a maid. In front of her is a gun that is attached to a clock whose hand is set to pull the trigger at noon. This scene of the helpless maid is crosscut with another showing the good guys apprehending the villain, then galloping to the rescue in a horse-drawn carriage. Seconds before the fatal hour, they jump through the window of the villain's lair, untie the maid, and save her. The film finishes with a bang.

We love this kind of ride, which is why over a century later we keep coming back for more.

Here's a closer look at another example of parallel action — the famous baptism scene from *The Godfather*. This sequence comes towards the end of the film: Michael Corleone has just succeeded as mafia godfather and while attending a baptism his men are all over town rubbing out the competition. The sequence runs to six pages and climaxes with:

```
CHURCH
The ceremony continues.


                    PRIEST'S VOICE
            Michael Francis Rizzi, do you
            renounce Satan?


While the church music continues:


CUT TO:


HOTEL ELEVATOR
Revealing Stracci, a Don, and the elevator
operator. The door opens and Clemenza fires two
shots.


CUT TO:

CHURCH
```

MICHAEL CORLEONE
    I do renounce him.

While the church music continues:

CUT TO:

MASSAGE ROOM
Gunman opens the door, Moe puts glasses on,
gets shot in one eye.

CUT TO:

CHURCH
                    PRIEST'S VOICE
    And all his works?

CUT TO:

HOTEL
Cicci ascending steps. Then follows Don Cuneo
into a revolving door, locks it, then shoots
four times through the glass.

CUT TO:

CHURCH
                    MICHAEL
    I do renounce them.

CUT TO:

MOTEL ROOM

Rocco kicks open the door and he and another gunman fire. The girl screams, "Oh God! Oh God!" as she and Tattaglia are riddled by bullets while in bed.

CUT TO:

CHURCH

                    PRIEST'S VOICE
    And all his pomps?

                    MICHAEL
    (nodding) I do renounce them.

CUT TO:

COURTHOUSE

Neri shoots Barzini's bodyguard twice, and his chauffeur once, as Barzini turns to run. Neri drops to one knee and carefully fires at Barzini, who topples after two shots. Neri gets picked up.

Although Peter Zinner must be credited for the editing, it was principally Coppola who both wrote and directed this sequence. Notice how he does away with conventional scene headings, uses the transition "Cut to," spills the church music across the murder scenes, and the brutal brevity of the action lines. This is parallel action, this is juxtaposition, this is great cinema. And it's clearly *writing for the cut.*

Action Scenes

When it comes to a fight scene the screenwriter might be expected to give just a short descriptor like, "Seconds later, Hit Girl is all over them" (*Kickass*). But for many big-budget action films, particularly those involving visual effects, writers might be expected to punch it out, blow by blow. So here again, the writer must *write for the cut*:

```
BOURNE — the lightbulb — he's tossing it
across the room — over her head — into that
frosted window and —


As she ducks down —


As it SHATTERS —


EVERYTHING STARTS HAPPENING AT ONCE


PHFT! — PHFT! — PHFT! — PHFT! — PHFT! — PHFT!
— silenced automatic weapons fire — raking into
the apartment and —


THE FROSTED WINDOW peppered with holes and —


MARIE on the floor as THE WINDOW SHATTERS above
her and —


CASTEL — he's in the airshaft! — hanging from
an abseil rope — but off-guard — FIRING BLIND —
strafing the apartment and —
```

BOURNE kicking that chair across the room and —

CASTEL reacting — instinct — moving target —

THE CHAIR just strafed to shit and —

This scene from *The Bourne Identity* is a kinetic poem. Screenwriters Tony Gilroy and William Herron write with the breathless, broken-speech quality of an eyewitness ducking bullets. It looks chaotic, but close up it's highly structured. Again, this is parallel action, but now the writers entirely dispense with the clutter of scene breaks. The cutting pattern is signaled in the line breaks, em dashes, and ellipses. Motion is suggested in the breathless tumble of exclamatory, present tense action lines. A sense of sequence and continuity is indicated by the repetition of "and" at the end of lines. And the focus of each "shot" is capitalized or placed at the front of the line; and where there are two in the same shot, the writers are happy to shuffle words out of order: "BOURNE — the lightbulb — he's tossing it across the room." There's even some sound design going on here — the *phft-phft-phft* of automatic gunfire.

Some action scenes compress time, some expand, and others do both. And this has much to do with film's extraordinary ability to mimic memory, dream, and trauma states. Famously, in the shower scene from *Psycho*, Hitchcock atomizes Marion's murder into a mosaic of short clips; from the moment Norman Bates draws back the curtain to the moment he leaves the bathroom, there are some thirty edits in a sequence that runs less than thirty seconds. Such frenetic editing effectively stretches the traumatic moment well beyond the bounds of real time.

Suspense

Writing good suspense is so clearly about understanding the motion and time qualities of editing. Suspense sequences are such an important feature of all kinds of movies, we're going to devote a little time to it here, and unpack some great examples.

If the first master of suspense was D.W. Griffith, then the next was Hitchcock, and then came Spielberg and many more. They were masters because they understood that suspense was the gift of editing. Here's Hitchcock:

> "I'm talking about the rules of suspense. That's why I've more or less had the field to myself. Selznick (Hollywood film producer) complained about what he called my 'goddamn jigsaw cutting.' I used to shoot the one piece of film in such a way that no one else could put the pieces together properly; the only way they could be edited was to follow exactly what I had in mind in the shooting stages." (*Hitchcock / Truffaut*)

So Hitchcock was a huge fan of editing. He encouraged his writers to *write for the cut*, he directed his films for the cut, he gives a demonstration of the Kuleshov Effect — he even married a film editor.

In conversation with François Truffaut, Hitchcock gives perhaps cinema's most famous definition of suspense. He tells the story of two characters enjoying an "innocent little chat," blissfully unaware of the danger they're in. The audience, on the other hand, knows that —

> "— the bomb is underneath the table . . . (and) is going to explode at one o'clock and there is a clock in the decor. In these conditions, the same innocuous conversation becomes fascinating because the public is participating in the scene. The audience is longing to warn the characters on the screen: 'You shouldn't be

talking about such trivial matters. There is a bomb beneath you and it is about to explode!'" (*Hitchcock / Truffaut*)

In practice, the engineers of the perfect suspense machine are editors; they decide the precise length of the shot, the moment to crosscut between the clock, the innocent chat, and the ticking bomb under the table. They will judge just how far they can stretch the viewer's nerve wires.

Spielberg had Hitchcock in mind when he was making his debut feature *Duel* —

"What I learned from Hitchcock is don't ever let the audience off the hook — be a whore about keeping the audience on tenter-hooks as long as possible before giving them some clue, or some kind of relief." (*Duel* — DVD extras)

SUSPENSE: BONNIE AND CLYDE

Let's look at the ambush scene from the 1967 movie *Bonnie and Clyde*. Here the viewer knows that Ivan, the father of one of the gang members, has set a trap (truck breakdown) on the road back to the hideout. We don't yet know where the "bomb" is — in this case bounty hunter Hamer and the lawmen — but they must be close by.

When Ivan flags down Bonnie and Clyde's car, there follows an innocent conversation: "I've got a flat tire, no spare." Then, in lieu of a literal clock, along the road from the opposite direction, comes a truck loaded with chickens. As the truck slowly approaches, Ivan begins to panic. The truck draws ever closer. Then *boom!* We are startled by an eruption in the bushes. No, it's not the lawmen, but two pheasants noisily taking flight. This is a classic "jump" moment — a faux explosion intended to wrong-foot the audience — "Wah! It's all kicking off! Oh no, it's not." In early gangster films, it might be a car backfiring, or a champagne cork popping seconds before the machine guns open fire.

So the pheasants explode out of the bushes, and now we can guess where the "bomb" is. Bonnie and Clyde watch the flight of the birds with unguarded surprise and wonder. Ivan's response is quite different — his anxiety is now at breaking point, he looks from the flying pheasants to the chicken truck, and back to the bush. And then he dives under his own truck to take cover. There follows a rapid cat's cradle of reaction shots as Bonnie and Clyde signal their "what the —?" puzzlement, their dreadful epiphany, and finally a farewell look of love. The lawmen open fire through the bushes.

There are many differences between the written scene compared to the more suspenseful movie sequence. In David Newman and Robert Benton's screenplay, the scene crosscuts between the unfolding action on the road, and the trench where the lawmen are visibly hiding — so the audience have no doubt about the jeopardy from the start. The chain reaction triggered by the pheasants is not in the screenplay. Instead, the bounty hunter, Hamer, stands up and calls to Clyde before the shooting starts. The shooting takes place off-camera as we observe the terrified reactions of the two men in the chicken truck; the action line reads, "It's over in seconds." In the film, as we know, the lawmen remain invisible, they open fire through the bushes, and the "ballet of blood" shooting goes on for over 35 seconds.

While the timing of parallel action will be largely down to the editor, when it comes to single location suspense sequences much of that precision engineering falls to the writer.

The Coen Brothers really know how to do this.

SUSPENSE: NO COUNTRY FOR OLD MEN

The filmmaking brothers Ethan and Joel Coen are rare in that they write, direct, and edit most of their films. Their knowledge of directing, and particularly editing, invests all their screenplays. They *write for the cut*. This is what Spike Jonze is admiring when he says:

> "I'm in awe of directors like the Coen Brothers, who can shoot their script and edit it, and that's the movie. They're not discovering the movie in postproduction. They're editing the script they shot." (*Vulture*)

We're going to look at the Eagle Hotel scene from the screenplay *No Country for Old Men*. This is an example of a suspense sequence where the timing of the "cut" falls to the writer because the scene unfolds in a single location. If you find this scene on YouTube, and read the script at the same time (there are PDFs floating around on the internet), you'll find yourself repeating what Spike Jonze just said.

The scene starts like this: It's night, and the protagonist Moss has checked into an out-of-season hotel, and lies awake on his bed wondering how the "angel of death" Anton Chigurh has been able to hunt him across the country. An idea strikes him; he sits up, opens the document case, and feels inside for a false bottom.

```
He starts riffling money packets.


He finds one that binds. It has hundreds on the
outside but ones inside with the centers cut
out. In the hollow is a sending unit the size
of a Zippo lighter.
```

He holds the sender, staring at it.

A long beat.

From somewhere, a dull chug. The sound is hard to read — a compressor going on, a door thud, maybe something else.

The sound has brought Moss's look up. He sits listening. No further sound.

Moss reaches to uncradle the rotary phone by the bed. He dials 0.

We hear ringing filtered through the handset. Also, faintly, offset, we hear the ring direct from downstairs.

After five rings, Moss cradles the phone.

He goes to the door, reaches for the knob, but hesitates.

He gets down on his hands and knees and listens at the crack under the door.

An open airy sound like a seashell put to your ear.

Moss rises and turns to the bed. He piles money back into the document case but freezes suddenly — for no reason we can see.

A long beat on his motionless back. We grad-
ually become aware of a faint high-fre-
quency beeping, barely audible. Its source is
indeterminate.

. . . Moss clasps the document case, picks up
his shotgun, and eases himself to a sitting
position on the bed, facing the door.

He looks at the line of light under it.

The beeps approach, though still not loud. A
long wait.

At length a soft shadow appears in the line of
light below the door. It lingers there. The
beeping-stops.

A beat. Now the soft shadow becomes more
focused. It resolves into two columns of dark:
feet planted before the door.

Moss raises his shotgun toward the door.
A long beat.

Moss adjusts his grip on the shotgun and his
finger tightens on the trigger.

The shadow moves, unhurriedly, rightward. The
band of light beneath the door is once again
unshadowed.

```
Quiet. Moss stares.

The band of light under the door.

Moss stares.

Silently, the light goes out.

Something for Moss to think about. He
stares . . .
```

This sequence is different from Hitchcock's bomb-under-the-table model. This time the hero knows as much as the audience — he's trapped in a room, and he knows the monster is getting closer. In this set-up, the viewer feels the same sense of rising tension, but instead of banging against an invisible window shouting, "Get out! Get out!" we're stuck in the room with Moss and keeping dead quiet.

The Coens have designed the "cutting pattern" to make a perfect suspense sequence. The rhythmic shot-reverse-shot editing is indicated in the line breaks; shot durations are signaled in the numerous time expansion cues (beat, long wait, Quiet, Something for Moss to think about, etc.). The bowstring of suspense is slowly pulled to breaking strain: by the end of the scene, it is dark in the bedroom, dark in the hallway, Moss's finger is tight on the trigger, and the demon is at the door. It is utterly silent and our collective "iris" is fully dilated. All is set for some *bing bang boom!*

We can also see here how a suspense scene inverts many of the defining characteristics of an action scene: time is stretched, movement is pent up, and sound cues are just audible. Kinesis is a pressure cooker with a faulty valve.

Dialogue for the cut

It may seem that much of what we're discussing is about action lines and scene breaks. But the cut goes deep into dialogue too. David Mamet captures this when he says:

> "If you listen to the way people tell stories, you will hear that they tell them cinematically. They jump from one thing to the next, and the story is moved along by a juxtaposition of images — which is to say, by the cut." (*On Directing Film*)

Mamet is suggesting the spoken word is like the cutting pattern found in movies. But this fragmentary way of talking is also quite literally how we write dialogue for film.

In the hands of a good writer, dialogue is action by other means. Two people talking to each other at a barroom table might strike us as an entirely inert way to start a film. But the writer is Aaron Sorkin and the film is *The Social Network*.

```
FROM THE BLACK WE HEAR —


                    MARK (V.O.)
          Did you know there are more people with
          genius IQ's living in China than there
          are people of any kind living in the
          United States?


                    ERICA (V.O.)
          That can't possibly be true.


                    MARK (V.O.)
          It is.
```

                    ERICA (V.O.)
What would account for that?

                    MARK (V.O.)
Well, first, an awful lot of people live
in China. But here's my question:

FADE IN:
INT. CAMPUS BAR — NIGHT

MARK ZUCKERBERG is a sweet-looking 19-year-
old . . . ERICA, also 19, is Mark's date . . .

                    MARK
How do you distinguish yourself in a
population of people who all got 1600 on
their SAT's?

                    ERICA
I didn't know they take SAT's in China.

                    MARK
They don't. I wasn't talking about China
anymore, I was talking about me.

                    ERICA
You got 1600?

                    MARK
Yes. I could sing in an a cappella group,
but I can't sing.

                    ERICA

Does that mean you actually got nothing
wrong?

                    MARK

I can row crew or invent a 25-dollar PC.

                    ERICA

Or you can get into a final club.

                    MARK

Or I can get into a final club.

                    ERICA

You know, from a woman's perspective,
sometimes not singing in an a cappella
group is a good thing?

                    MARK

This is serious.

                    ERICA

On the other hand I do like guys who row
crew.
                    MARK
                   (beat)
Well I can't do that.

                    ERICA

I was kid —

                              MARK

              Yes, it means I got nothing wrong on
              the test.

                              ERICA

              Have you ever tried?

                              MARK

              I'm trying right now.

                              ERICA

              To row crew?

                              MARK

              To get into a final club. To row crew? No.
              Are you, like — whatever — delusional?

Surprising, energized words flow in the dark obliging the audience to play catch-up. The dialogue has the rat-a-tat-tat timing of a comedy double-act. This is editing made verbal: the conversation is strongly rhythmical, laconic, and the dialogue threads are deliberately shuffled (disjunctions around SATs, row crew, and final club; the question "You got nothing wrong?" is only answered eight exchanges later).

In Margaret Mehring's screenwriting manual *The Screenplay: A Blend of Film Form and Content*, she directly relates the writing of dialogue to the cut:

> "Dialogue contributes to editorial motion through rhythm, tempo, and pacing. Dialogue has rhythm in its repetition of words, ideas, and manner of speech. It develops tempo through the length of speech patterns."

Sorkin began his dialogue-as-action project as the writer of *A Few Good Men* in 1992, and later we saw it flourish in the TV series *The West Wing* (1999–2006). Here, highly choreographed scenes would feature characters walking at speed along the White House corridors, seemingly colliding with colleagues for terse, quick-fire verbal exchanges. These would be long takes with no edits; the kinetic energy of the cut is transferred to the walk and the talk. One finds much the same dynamic at play in films such as *American Hustle*, the "single-take" film *Birdman*, and many of the screenplays of David Mamet, Quentin Tarantino, and others.

Here's another example, this time from John Hodge's *T2 Trainspotting*. We're in a grim bar in Glasgow: Renton and Simon meet for the first time twenty years after Renton double-crossed him and ran off with their ill-gotten loot.

SIMON

Well, hello, Mark.

RENTON

Simon.

They sit. It seems cordial, if barbed.

SIMON

So, what you been up to? For twenty years.

RENTON

Oh, where to start? I've been in Amsterdam.

                    SIMON

          Nice.

                    RENTON

          It's all right.

                    SIMON

          What else? Married?

                    RENTON

          Dutch woman.

                    SIMON

          Kids?

          A fraction of a second hesitation

                    RENTON

          Two.

                    SIMON

          Aaaw! Boys or girls?

                    RENTON

          One of each.

                    SIMON

          Lovely. Wee Mark, eh? I'll bet he's a
          chip off the old block.

```
                    RENTON
      James, actually. And Laura. How about
      you?


                    SIMON
      I have a son. He's in London with his
      fucking hoor mother.
```

This is the rhythm of the cut punched out in monosyllables. A "fraction of a second" is enough to signal "lie" or "don't want to say," and it effectively breaks the rhythm from trading jabs to a blocking move. And then the dialogue shifts into longer combination punches. And this verbal bout prefigures the vicious punch-up that happens twenty seconds later.

Exercises

1. For a classic Hitchcockian suspense scene, check out the brick-in-the-satchel moment in Fran Walsh / Peter Jackson's screenplay *Heavenly Creatures*: Pauline and Juliet enter Honorah Rieper's kitchen and have an innocent conversation . . . (you can find the screenplay online). Then take a fresh look at the suspense scenes in your screen story — can you add some Hitch?

2. Let's recall Margaret Mehring's observation: "Dialogue contributes to the editorial motion through rhythm, tempo, and pacing." Now find the screenplay for *American Hustle* online. Look for the first dialogue scene where Richie DiMaso is saying: "What are you doing, going

behind my back? Telling people I'm screwing up this operation?" As you read, consider how editing is made verbal.

Check some of your own dialogue scenes; do they "dance"?
Break it up, make some rhythms — play with it.

CHAPTER 8

CITY OF GOD

*A case study — the opening sequence to a film
that captures most of our editing moves*

"And . . . action, Rooster. OK, now, you're being tied up so look
bothered . . . good. Woah — they're sharpening a big knife —
you're anxious! Great! Ok now look over there — yeah — see
they're putting the water on to boil — you're going in the cooking pot — you're frightened out of your feathers . . . you bet!
And cut!"

We're going to look in some detail at the opening sequence of *City
of God* because it features an Oscar-winning performance from
a rooster, and because Bráulio Mantovani's screenplay so clearly
shimmies to the music of the cut. Specifically it demonstrates: substitution splice, suspense, parallel action, in medias res, and script-
planned montage.

The film opens with a frightened rooster. How do we know the
rooster is frightened? David Mamet explains how this works by
reference to natural history documentaries:

"Documentaries take basically unrelated footage and juxtapose it
in order to give the viewer the idea the filmmaker wants to convey. They take footage of birds snapping a twig. They take footage
of a fawn raising his head. The two shots have nothing to do with
each other. They are not a record of what the protagonist did.

They're basically uninflected images. But they give the viewer the idea of alertness to danger when they are juxtaposed. That's good filmmaking." (*On Directing Films*)

Otherwise known as the Kuleshov Effect. Now let's look at how Mantovani wrote the opening sequence of *City of God*.

SECTION 1: SUSPENSE

A big KNIFE being sharpened. Super: 1981 The murmur of HAPPY voices is heard, voices SINGING a samba accompanied by a banging drum. We can't see the people but it sounds like a festive environment.	
BLACK HANDS tethers the LEG of a magnificent ROOSTER.	
The ROOSTER looks bothered at having his leg tied up.	

WATER BOILING in an enormous pan.	
The ROOSTER seems to react to the previous shot.	
Potatoes being peeled by the HANDS of a black woman.	
The ROOSTER reacts as if it knows what's going on: he's going to be lunch.	
The HANDS of black women pluck the feathers of DEAD CHICKENS.	

The ROOSTER reacts. He tries to escape but his leg is tethered.	
A black HAND beats a tambourine.	
The ROOSTER seems to understand his end is near.	
A big KNIFE being sharpened.	
The ROOSTER is desperate — it struggles —	

The film drops us into the middle of things; we're in a sudden world of fiesta, music, and food, and we're seeing this world in fragments from the anxious point of view of a rooster. Our hero is tethered, visibly frightened, and heading for the cooking pot.

This is what Mamet was talking about. On the day of the shoot, they tethered the rooster and they filmed it doing what roosters do; the usual head jerking, pecking, scratching stuff. By placing the camera at rooster-height, and using POV juxtapositions with images of knives, cooking pots, and dead chickens, the rooster's plight is anthropomorphized; the viewer believes the rooster really understands its own peril and is showing signs of mounting anxiety. "I'm very scared — how do I get out of here — I'm going to die!" Mamet might call this "uninflected acting," allowing the cut to signal the meaning, the emotion, and subtext. Think Ryan Gosling.

So the hero has been tied up, and is made to watch his comrades die a ghastly death knowing that he too will go the same way: this is a classic suspense sequence. Every line of the script signals a cut, and every cut ratchets up the suspense: the tether, the knife, the cooking pot, the vegetables, the knife again, the slaughter of chickens. This rhythmic cutting pattern — rooster-watching > POV of impending doom > rooster-reacting — is the "ticking" of the clock. Mantovani even gives us a signature "jump" moment with the beating of a tambourine.

And this rooster-world is presented as a puzzle; the usual orientation descriptors of *who* and *where* are deliberately withheld — "we can't see the people" — they are initially only revealed through close-ups of their busy hands. We're given a wealth of sound cues: samba music, the murmur of happy voices, the rasping of knife on stone, chopping and peeling.

SECTION 2: THE CHASE — PARALLEL ACTION —
AND WELCOME TO THE CITY OF GOD

The ROOSTER is desperate — it struggles —	
— and escapes.	

ALMEIDINHA, the guy holding the knife, sees the ROOSTER got away and gives the alarm.
 	
         ALMEIDINHA
   The rooster ran off!
 	
Now for the first time we see Almeidinha's house. It's a poor brick place in the City of God. The party's happening in the garden.

The escaped ROOSTER prompts a lot of excitement amongst the guests — mostly young men, BLACKS, MULATTOS, and some WHITES. Almost all of them in shorts and flip-flops.	

Dozens of these bandits
run after the ROOSTER.
They're all part of L'il
Zé's gang. Everyone's
shouting —

        BANDITS' VOICES
   Grab the rooster, grab
   the rooster!

EXT. NEARBY STREET — DAY
ROCKET, the narrator
of the story, holds a
professional stills camera
in his hand. He's black
and maybe 18 years old.
Next to him is his friend
STRINGY.

They walk down the street
together.

        STRINGY
   Hey Rocket, do you
   really think they'll
   give you the job at the
   paper if you take that
   photo?

        ROCKET
   I have to risk it.

        STRINGY
   Bro, you'd risk your
   life just for a photo?
   Forget it!

```
PARALLEL ACTION
We interweave the
conversation between
Stringy and Rocket with
images of the bandits
chasing the ROOSTER down
the alleys of the City of
God.
```

With the rooster's escape, suspense is over, and the chase begins. Now the information withheld in the first section is revealed — we're no longer in the world of the rooster, we're in the world of men. Mantovani gives brief orientation descriptors about the location, the people, and the party. This section is clearly more about setup than the cut. Though these descriptors run to over 70 words, in fact there is no break in the action — the rooster has escaped, the shout goes up, and the gang rush after it.

There is a scene break, we cut to a nearby street, and we're suddenly in the company of two young men in the middle of a casual conversation. In a blink, we've jumped from a noisy, wild chase to a quiet, ambling scene: two friends talking, and the first real dialogue of the film. And the audience is playing catch-up. *Who are these guys? Are they talking about photography? Did he just say, "Risk your life for a photo"?* This abrupt juxtaposition (mob rush, shouting / couple, ambling dialogue) has an intentionally jolting effect on the viewer.

And then with the words "parallel action" Mantovani makes it clear this jolt is not a one-off but is the beginning of the fairground ride he's building.

For the sake of brevity I have omitted several more "catch that rooster" scenes that are exciting in themselves but also cunningly serve to introduce us to the favela ("simple houses, very poor streets") and the locals ("most of the residents are black, poor, and scared"). These for-the-cut scenes are a familiar movie device; they recall the chase scene near the beginning of *Slumdog Millionaire* where the two kids Salim and Amir are chased by a cop through the slums of Juhu — again serving as a "welcome to the world of the slums." In *City of God*, they are interwoven with further dialogue scenes with Rocket and Stringy where they're still discussing taking a photo of a dangerous gangster.

SECTION 3: PARALLEL ACTION, A NEW SUSPENSE SEQUENCE — THE STAKES ARE RAISED

As L'il Zé rounds a corner, he bumps into a PAN SELLER and falls on top of the pans.

He gives a loud, high-pitched laugh, gets up, and violently BEATS the PAN SELLER.

L'il Zé grabs a GUN from the back of his shorts. It looks like he's going to kill the poor guy. Instead, he points it in the air and shouts:
 	
        L'IL ZÉ
   Drill that rooster!

Immediately all the bandits get their guns out and run after the ROOSTER who's now at the far end of the street.	

STREET — ROCKET AND STRINGY
 	
       STRINGY
  Fuck this — let it go. If you find the guy, he'll kill you.
 	
       ROCKET
  Stringy — the last thing I want is to come face to face with that hood.

Here's an obvious difference between reading the script and watching the film: the reader has been told about L'il Zé, and we've seen the word "gang" and "bandit" several times. But a viewer watching the film at the cinema can know very little of this, and so far the chase has just looked like high-spirited fun. Mantovani now sets a bomb ticking in three quick moves; L'il Zé bumps into a pan seller and beats him (aw — bit harsh); he then takes out a gun and it looks like he's going to shoot the guy (woah!). And then he shouts to the mob, "Drill the rooster," and in a blink the whole mob are toting guns (wtf!). From here, this parallel action sequence takes on the trappings of a second suspense sequence. When we cut back to Rocket, Stringy, and their "innocent conversation," we feel the electricity of doom bearing down on them. In fact their conversation is innocent in both the Hitchcockian sense of, "Get out of there. You don't know the danger you're in!" and ironic in that L'il Zé is the very gangster Rocket and Stringy have been talking about.

SECTION 4: THE BOMB IS STILL TICKING, AND THEN A SECOND BOMB SHOWS UP

At that moment, the two parallel actions meet — the ROOSTER goes around the corner.

Behind it appear L'il Zé and his gang.

Stringy opens his eyes wide. Rocket lifts his camera but stops halfway. He's paralyzed — L'il Zé points the gun at Rocket and shouts:

> L'IL ZÉ
> Grab the rooster!

Rocket crouches down like a goalie. Awkwardly he tries to grab the ROOSTER, but it runs between his legs.

A WOMAN walking with her pram sees the scene and quickly moves away.

L'il Zé walks forward. Rocket looks scared. Stringy is paralyzed.

L'il Zé suddenly stops. All the bandits point their guns to someone behind Rocket.

Rocket looks behind him and sees a PATROL of 6 policemen. In front of the patrol is Detective Cabeçao — northern and evil looking.

Rocket is still in the same pose of clumsy goalie. The picture freezes.

> ROCKET (V.O.)
> In the City of God, you can't know what's worse: dealing with the bandits or the police. If you run away, they get you. If you stay, they get you too. It's been that way ever since I was a kid . . .

```
EXT. SMALL FOOTBALL
CAMP — DAY
A small group of boys aged
8—10 years old is playing
football. Among them are
Rocket and Stringy.

Super: The '60s
Rocket is crouching as a
goalie.
```

In this last section, the two worlds collide, but the bomb doesn't go off. We get a new time signature: Stringy opens his eyes wide, Rocket lifts his camera but stops half way, L'il Zé points the gun at Rocket, and A WOMAN walking with her pram sees the scene and quickly moves away. This is written as a Western showdown. The interweaving rush of the last few scenes has signaled a sense of inevitable disaster for the two boys; at the moment of collision, the kinetic pulse appears to stop. But it's actually coiling. (In the film, director Fernando Meirelles gives us two quite stylized shots: L'il Zé arriving in slow motion, and Rocket gets a 90-degree camera spin that ends in slow motion as he registers who's just shown up.)

"Grab the rooster!" we've heard this a few times before, but now addressed to Rocket by a guy pointing a gun, you know it's not an invitation to come and play. Rocket crouches in the pose of a goalie, but the rooster runs through his legs.

Then that coil of suspense gets three more twists: L'il Zé moves forward, Rocket looks scared, and Stringy is paralyzed. And then a puzzle: L'il Zé stops in his tracks, and the mob seem to have refocused on another target.

We turn with Rocket to discover the cops lined up at the opposite end of the street. The action lines here suggest a wide shot of the police squad, to mid-shot of an individual, finishing on a close-up of the detective's face. The police have arrived, but we can tell this is definitely not a yay-it's-the-cavalry! moment: the symmetry in the lineup of L'il Zé's gang and the police intentionally equates the two. The clumsy goalie is trapped in the middle of a double doom. And just as this second bomb starts ticking, all goes silent: Mantovani uses a postproduction device: a freeze-frame. Now this victim-in-the-middle image becomes a kind of emblem, a pause to allow us to listen to Rocket's thoughts in voiceover. And as Rocket refers back to his childhood, so in a blink we're transported back to a football pitch in the '60s. Adult goalie > cut > child goalie: a substitution splice.

In these first three pages, the images, sounds, and cutting pattern of the movie jump off the page. Mantovani has written a for-the-cut overture that clearly states the style, structure, and mood of the entire film. It also metaphorically and literally states the theme of the film: "You're dead if you run away, you're dead if you stay."

This is a bravura piece of writing and filmmaking. It may seem that many of the examples I've given so far are all similarly show-boat-y. And it's true to say writing for the cut shouts loudest at these moments; but be in no doubt, this is the animating force of the entire screenplay.

Exercises

On YouTube, find the opening sequence of *Don't Look Now* (up to the scream).

Now, write that sequence as a kind of "beat poem" (the story beats of the sequence).

For example, this is my beat poem for *City of God* — I'm trying to capture the rhythm and pattern of what I'm seeing:

Black
Knife rasps across a whetstone
Black
The rooster is watching
Knife rasps across a whetstone
Festive music, someone shaking maracas
Black
Hands peeling carrots, feet dancing
Knife rasps across a whetstone
The rooster is tethered — no escape
Knife slits chicken's throat
The rooster is frightened
Fire lit under a huge cooking pot
Chicken plucked and butchered
Feathers fall — the rooster knows he's next
A hand swipes across a guitar, beer flows
The rooster so anxious
Chicken pieces thrown in the cooking pot
The rooster strains at his tether.

Once you've written the beat poem, see to what degree you can now write the opening scenes of *Don't Look Now* using the conventional screenplay format without losing any of the suggestive, puzzle, kinetic qualities of your poem.

CHAPTER 9

TORPEDO BOAT

*The story so far, arthouse versus mainstream,
to cut or not to cut*

IN *SUNSET BOULEVARD*, during screenwriter Joe Gillis's first encounter with movie star Norma Desmond, she asks him:

>   NORMA
>   And you have written pictures,
>   haven't you?
>
>   GILLIS
>   Sure have. The last one I wrote was about
>   cattle rustlers. Before they were through
>   with it, the whole thing played on a tor-
>   pedo boat.

Sheesh — the things they do to our stories. Studio meddling and "visionary" producers can bend a story out of whack before it's even gotten into production. And then out there on location — the vagaries of performance, direction, location, wardrobe, and the weather will all significantly add and subtract to your story.

What can we do about any of that? How do we write stories that are proof against the violence of the money, the shoot, and the cut?

The fact is we can't, and we shouldn't expect to.

A screenplay is a proposal, a statement of intent — it really isn't a blueprint. However if we are *writing for the cut* we are increasing the "moviness" of our story. It's this quality in the writing that projects the story as a fully formed movie in the imagination of the director, cinematographer, designer, actor, and editor. And if this is happening, then your screenplay will not only survive production, but will flourish as all those creatives will be working to enhance your story. Instead of building a torpedo boat.

We've come some way on this *writing for the cut* expedition, so now would be a good moment to summarize this thing. And then give it a good kick.

In a nutshell

Writing for the cut means writing in images and sounds with editing in mind. It aligns the screenplay with the way movies are actually made, capturing the dance of the edit in the writing. We have identified a number of for-the-cut strategies screenwriters can use. However, what we're describing is probably more a sensibility than a method.

All professional screenwriters *write for the cut*. Probably most would just call it screenwriting.

This juxtapositional way of writing both animates and "tells" the story. It obliges the viewer to make sense of the cut and, in so doing, contribute to the unfolding of the story. In this way, the film does not explain the story, but rather we "discover" it for ourselves.

Juxtapositions prompt the viewer to contribute to the story in different ways. This juxtapositional effect can be thought of as axes:

Suggestion > Statement
Puzzle > Exposition
Kinesis > Stasis

From this, I've shaken out a number of cut strategies for screenwriters: substitution splice, split scene break, nonlinear shuffle, ellipsis, in medias res, script-planned montage, opening / title sequence, action, parallel action, suspense, and dialogue.

Nut cracker

So let's flip this on its head and ask: Can we write for the big screen in a way that is absolutely not for the cut? Asking this question allows us to look at alternative strategies, and to give *writing for the cut* a good bash to see if it holds up.

As suggested earlier, if we're arriving fresh to screenwriting the tendency may be to write for a *notion* of cinema. This is a bit like making your favorite cake from memories of its flavor, smell, and appearance. We might get some way with this "notion approach," but even if the story is strong, it will struggle to make the jump into production.

Similarly, we may set off with an idea we're writing for cinema, but we're actually writing literature. From our school days, the way we've learned and practiced writing stories leans toward narrative continuity, rounded sentences, psychological musings, and good grammar. And that isn't like screenwriting at all.

Alexander Mackendrick has some thoughts on this subject. A celebrated director from the glory days of Ealing Studios, he later became a seminal teacher at CalArts. Here's an extract from a letter to one of his film students:

"That you have some facility as a writer is very clear, what I don't understand is why you have come to a film school. Your literary facility is your chief handicap in writing for the screen . . . I will absolutely refuse to accept from you the kind of writing in which descriptive charm is indulged in order to evade the much harder task of putting on paper only what can be seen or heard, what is concrete, specific. This will be a kind of castration for you, I realize, but I know of no other way of forcing you to confront a fundamental difference between writing that is meant to be read, and the task of thinking in movie terms." (*YouTube: Mackendrick On Film*)

It may be the film student followed his advice and went on to write *Thelma and Louise*. Or it may be she ignored everything Mackendrick said and wrote *My Dinner With Andre*. (If you don't know this film, it goes like this: two friends talk to each other at a restaurant table. And they're talking about life, things they've done, their different worldviews. And um . . . that's what they do for the entire film, right there at the dinner table.)

Mackendrick is spitting fire. But as we know *My Dinner with Andre* became a cult classic.

Thankfully, cinema is a really broad church, and there are many, many outliers. And wherever film movements seem to congregate around a set of codes and conventions, there will be a sharp reaction against it. And that reaction will often deliver to the world a fantastic variety of exotics, madcaps, and politicos. The best of these films will be special precisely because they do not provide models for others to follow; often they're a kind of signature of the director.

If we are writing for commercial cinema, we should be very interested in what goes on next door in the arthouse.

I once overheard a conversation in a cinema queue, and it went something like: "Arthouse films? They make me tired. They're slow, they don't make sense, don't make money, and the actors are funny-looking."

In the nature of an experiment, arthouse can deliver both the radically new and the devastatingly awful. There is much to be learned either way — so eat it all up.

To cut or not to cut?

No one would want to generalize about arthouse. It's not a genre, and it's as wide as the sky. But one enduring feature of some arthouse movies is the "long take." That includes films like *Code Unknown*, *Before Sunrise*, *The Thief, The Cook, His Wife & Her Lover*, *Songs from the Second Floor*, *The Sacrifice*, and films in the tradition of directors like Jean Renoir and Alain Resnais. At its most extreme, it's films like *Rope*, *Russian Ark*, and *Birdman* which play out without a single (apparent) cut. All these films seem to confound the storytelling idea of *writing for the cut*. So how do they work?

In broad terms, many of these films displace the dynamics of the cut into the dialogue, the performance, the choreography of the actors, the movement of the camera, or the sheer "otherness" of the content. Hitchcock looks like the odd man out in this lineup of arthouse directors. But *Rope* is an interesting case. Hitchcock had seen *Rope* performed in the theatre as a real-time, continuous action play, and he wondered if he could replicate this feat for the big screen. In later years, Hitchcock rather regretted the experiment:

> "When I look back, I realize that it was quite nonsensical because I was breaking with my own theories on the importance of cutting and montage for the visual narration of the story." (*Hitchcock / Truffaut*)

But this interest in real-time action and a sense of theatre can be found in a number of long-take movies. In both *Code Unknown* and *The Thief, The Cook*, for example, real-time scenes are punctuated by short intervals of black — the equivalent of the theatre curtain going up and down. On the face of it, this approach takes us right back to Méliès' *Cinderella*, a theatre-movie hybrid he made in 1899. But on closer inspection, we can see there's something else going on.

Look at Haneke's "subway attack" scene in *Code Unknown*. Here's a scene that runs for five and a half minutes without a cut. A single camera captures events: Anna Laurent (Juliette Binoche) is a person in the crowd at the far end of a subway carriage. Two youths get on the train, and one of them entertains his friend with a sexually humiliating verbal assault on Anna. She gets up and moves to the front of the carriage close to where the camera has been set. The boy follows her and continues his sadistic game. Everyone in the carriage is looking the other way. As the boy stands to get off the train, he spits in Anna's face. An older passenger squares up to the boy. We're only at the midpoint, and the tension continues to mount for another two and a half minutes (look for the clip on YouTube).

Haneke delivers a deeply upsetting and perfectly crafted suspense scene without a single cut. All of the storytelling is in the shot: the choreography, the timing of small but significant events, the dialogue, and the pitch-perfect performances. The camera holds a wide, virtually static shot throughout. A long take in this context has a special power, and that power resides in the flip side of the cut. As a viewer, we are long-habituated to the conventions of screen storytelling — we expect a cut. And when it doesn't come, we feel a prickling sense of unease (something is wrong). Everything about the look and feel of this scene borrows from a tradition of acute observational documentary making, and an association with the "real." Haneke wanted to evoke in the viewer a sense of voyeurism, rather as if we were one of the scared passengers looking the other way. Except that he makes us watch, and the longer we watch, the more acutely we feel a sense complicity and imminent violence.

Another famous arthouse filmmaker Andrei Tarkovsky rejected the editing theories of Kuleshov and Eisenstein. In his book *Sculpting in Time*, he writes about the rhythmic and time pressures in the film segments. For him, editing is not so much a juxtapositional process, but more a kind of plumbing in which the shots need to be correctly joined so that time is allowed to flow.

Yay — this is great! I love his films!

So let's say I want to write a Tarkovsky-like screenplay of long takes. At the beginning of my first scene, I write: "This scene plays out in a single take, like one of those Tarkovsky films." OK I can see that's not going to work. At my next attempt, I suggest the unblinking quality of a long-take scene by writing sentences that run on and on without comma or full stop but this will not look pretty so can you stop now please.

You want to write long-take films? Then you can be like Tarkovsky, or any director you love, and make the film yourself. And you can do this. You really can.

At the other end of the scale, there are legions of auteur filmmakers who are happy to make long and short-take movies, and celebrate the storytelling power of the cut.

Robert Bresson who wrote and directed *Pickpocket* and *L' Argent*, for example, says:

"An image must be transformed by contact with other images, as is a color by contact with other colors. A blue is not the same blue beside a green, a yellow, a red." (*Notes on Cinematography*)

And then there's Godard.

New Wave filmmaker Jean-Luc Godard and cine-theorist Andrew Bazin famously went head to head in 1956 over this vexed question of film storytelling: to cut or not to cut. At the time Godard was breaking all the rules about editing, cutting where you're not supposed to, and using this new thing — a "jump cut" — which got everyone sitting up straight in their seats. Bazin didn't like it. Godard didn't care.

They wrote essays.

Andre Bazin burst out of his corner with *Editing Prohibited*, and Godard came back swinging with *Editing, My Beautiful Concern*.

Here's Bazin grinding his teeth: "A sizeable portion of the public, if you asked them to concentrate a little, would be able to distinguish between real scenes and those created by editing." Real scenes are ones that are somehow complete in themselves; for Bazin mise-en-scene (film storytelling) was everything but the cut.

Goddard was unrepentant. In his essay, he says, "Editing is above all an integral part of mise-en-scene . . . If direction is a look, editing is a heartbeat." (*Cahier du Cinema*)

I'd say Bazin's argument is correct for a fraction of arthouse films, and Godard's argument is correct for the rest of arthouse films, and for nearly every commercial film that has ever been made on earth. And on planets we have yet to discover.

Can the cut really tell the story?

I want to finish this chapter by asking this big question again. If we're going to *write for the cut*, we need to be absolutely convinced it has narrative effect.

As a screenwriter thinking about our choices for a new film story, we have a galaxy of possibilities; we are overwhelmed. Now let's look at the editor's range of operations.

Editors can cut shots together (sound and picture), they can dissolve one shot with another shot, and they can split the cut so that sound arrives ahead of the picture, or the picture arrives ahead of the sound. They can insert a shot into another shot (a cutaway such as a reaction shot). They can insert "filler" between shots or at the front and end of the film (filler is also known as slug, black, and spacer). In addition to synchronous sounds such as dialogue, editors can add different kinds of audio such as voiceover narration, music, and sound effects. And that's just about it.

Seems quite meager compared to what we can do with words and story worlds. But that's because editors are not inventing story, they're telling it. And from this seemingly small pool of operations, an abundance of narrative possibilities open up; parallel action, continuity and discontinuity, text and subtext, ellipses, expansion and contraction of time, pattern and rhythm, flashback, dream sequences, and multiple plotlines.

Writers are rarely found in the cutting room. But for those who have enjoyed that rare privilege of watching an editor at work, their writing is often changed forever. The author Michael Ondaatje observed Walter Murch cutting the film adaptation of his book *The English Patient*, and he imagined the thought processes of the editor:

"Can we eliminate that detour to the oasis scene completely? Can we leap the next three minutes and nestle this moment with that moment, thereby bonding two scenes that are strangers? How to avoid a series of plot bottlenecks, how to influence or 'save' a scene in the fifty-third minute of the film by doing something very small in the seventh, how to double the tension by doubling the sense of silence or not cutting away to that knife at all. How, even, to disguise the fact that an essential scene was never shot." (*The Conversations*)

The fact is, virtually no one apart from the director is invited into the edit suite. We just don't know what goes on behind that closed door. There are very few editor accounts of cutting a movie; for reasons of commercial sensitivity and professional prudence, editors simply can't talk about the specifics of their work. Which is why Ralph Rosenblum's book *When the Shooting Stops . . . the Cutting Begins: A Film Editor's Story* is a rare treasure. Rosenblum gives several frank and detailed accounts of films he has "fixed" in the edit. Perhaps the most startling are the chapters devoted to editing *The Night They Raided Minsky's* and *Annie Hall*. Here, in forensic detail, he shows how in postproduction the editor can effectively "write" a new story from the rushes.

CHAPTER 10

THE LIE DETECTOR

The dark side — the "gap of fit" between word and moving image, and how editing reveals and fixes flaws

THIS IS A TRUE STORY about a thriller film called *Monkey Time* (I've changed the name to protect the innocent). Three editors cut this film. This film went badly wrong — the number of editors is a clue.

Monkey Time was written by an A-list screenwriter. When the screenplay did the rounds, everyone thought it was wonderful. It was greenlit, a dream team of talent was assembled, and $80 million was invested.

There's a six-month shoot; all goes well. Then the director and all the film rushes fetch up in a small dark room with the editor. The editor begins to cut the material. After a month or so, she comes home late one night looking a bit down.

Her husband says, "Hi hon, what's up?"

She says, "The story doesn't work."

And he says, "Oh."

There's a test screening at a New York cinema; the audience finds the story confusing and gives it one of the lowest ratings ever recorded. The exec producer orders several recuts, hates all of them. He recuts the film himself; hates that, too. He hires a new film editor. Another director is drafted in to help the first director. They change about 40% of the original story, and spend a month on reshoots. At the next test screening, the new version fares only slightly better than the first. The film never makes it to cinema, and is chucked in the video stream, where it's chewed up by the critics.

It's taken four years to complete, the final budget exceeds $100 million, the film is poor, and everyone's reputation is in tatters.

The story doesn't work? How can that be? Everyone agreed the screenplay was a triumph on the printed page. But in the translation to the screen, it fell apart.

This is an illustration of the gap of fit between word and moving image. When you're reading a script, you're clearly not seeing the film. But there's a further complication here: *Monkey Time* like many screenplays by A-list writers, was received with such reverence it just didn't get the scrutiny it so clearly needed.

Editing is a beautiful, alchemical craft. But it has a dark side: editing is a lie detector. It detects acting lies, directing lies, dialogue lies, and cinematography lies. But the biggest lie it detects is the flaw in the story.

A screenplay, which is a simple text document, may attract millions in investment. And yet this investment is made with no clear proof that the story will still be breathing after the shoot and the cut. Those test screenings of *Monkey Time* in New York — they took place *after* the money was spent. Too late.

So editing is a lie detector; whatever is "wrong" in the script or the shoot becomes brutally exposed in the cutting room. It's a kind of diagnostic tool that can reveal: "These shots / this sequence / this dialogue / this performance / this story doesn't work." And it is also a fixing tool: "If we condense this scene, extend this shot, remove this character, change the scene order, and create a montage here — we can save Act 2!" (In reality, the business of "saving the film in post" is rarely quite as eureka as this.)

Returning to the ill-fated *Monkey Time,* here's what the third editor, let's call him Danny, said:

> "When a big director and a big writer get together to make a film, there's very little analysis of the script — it's all about reputations . . . it's as if no one actually sat down and read the script and asked, 'Is this good?' A thriller has to be so watertight — it has to be like an equation."

Danny relates that, after the abysmal 20% satisfaction rating at the New York test screening, a second big-name director was asked to help the first director. The idea was for the directors and the editor to huddle in the edit suite to salvage what they could and see what new story they might tell.

> "We went through the entire film taking out dialogue, whole characters, while thinking about new plots we'd need to write. We chucked 40% of the movie in the bin. I replaced all those scenes with black title cards showing new dialogue between characters and new scenes to be written . . . The director created a new love story that was never in the script, and a whole story strand was removed . . . Once it was written and they shot those parts it was pretty easy to put it all together, because it was so tailored for the 'black holes.'"

This whole wasteful process is very interesting to me. It's like rapid prototyping gone wrong — fixing the design after the product has been manufactured. Also, it's not rapid. When I looked into this and spoke to more editors, I discovered this gone-wrong-prototyping is relatively common, particularly with really big-budget movies. Listen to a couple of my interviewees talking. First a blockbuster editor:

"I'd say the bigger the budget the looser the script because they're giving themselves just loads of fucking options in the edit . . . I happen to know the shooting draft of *The Amazing Spider-Man 2* was about 180 pages, and the first cut was nearly five hours. So a lot gets jettisoned — they don't really know the film they're making . . ."

And this from a guy that does previsualizations for big action movies:

"I've seen it on a lot of films where you're in the cutting room. OK, the director's done his director's cut, he's had six weeks, he's now obligated to show this to the producers and the studio. And it's two hours and fifty minutes long and it's meant to be a ninety-minute movie. And everyone's saying, 'What the fuck are you doing?' The director's introduced like an hour and twenty minutes of additional material, subplots, characters, and development — and now you've got to take it out. It's just fucking crazy. And so the editor is fired and the director is kicked out of the cutting room. And the new editor ends up cutting with the producer. And that never turns out a good movie. It's just a dumb way of making a movie."

If we were looking for a better model of film production, we'd first want to remove the dumb. Then we'd want to start from the ground up and really test the movie-worthiness of the screenplay before principal photography began.

In a sense, most studios do this when they get into storyboarding. Once a movie has been greenlit, and before the shoot, the storyboard artist will often visualize the whole screenplay in line drawings. This may incidentally reveal problems, but the storyboard artist has no remit to probe or test the storytelling. In a way, the artist could be adding to the corporate delusion: *We're all going to make a movie as beautiful as these illustrations.*

You'd think an obvious way to test the screenplay before the shoot is give it to a movie editor. They're going to have to deal with the harvest of this screenplay — surely they'd see the flaws? And sometimes directors do this, and sometimes they don't. Anne Coates said:

"When you read the script, you think, 'Oh, well. They probably won't shoot that,' and then they do. And when you do cut those scenes out they mostly don't mind . . . But it's something they can't seem to take out at that early stage. And I know as the editor it's not going to be in the final cut."

Here's an editor of action movies talking:

"When I read the first draft of the script, I put my finger on two massive scenes towards the end of the second act; a sequence on an oil rig, and another set in Morocco — huge set pieces, big expense. I said, 'Guys, you're going to waste your money. By all means shoot this, but neither of these scenes are ever going to be in the film.'"

And because the director trusted the editor, these scenes were cut before production, saving possibly millions from the budget.

More commonly, this kind of discussion between director and editor will form part of the hiring process. And this would tend to make the editor a little cautious. Here's Walter Murch:

"I will write notes, usually 6 to 10 pages: 'I loved this . . . I was confused here . . . this might be redundant, but I don't know what you have in mind, Mr. Director.' Or sometimes it'll be, 'I have an idea which I'm going to toss to you — a way to do this completely differently — take it for what it's worth.' Sometimes the director says, 'Great, this is fantastic.' Other times — in not these words — they'll say, 'I don't think we should work together.'"

It's also fair to say movie editors can be brilliant at their craft, but make poor script readers. After all, this isn't really their thing. They don't trade in words.

So how can we screenwriters test before the shoot? Imagine you could somehow write your screenplay in the cutting room. Imagine you could apply some of the alchemy, economy, and lie detection of the cut while you were writing your script. In the next chapter, we explore this some more.

Exercises

Learn to edit drama. I'm serious — start now. Don't think about it — jump in.

Editing software is free or cheap, it's probably already sitting on your computer. You can get up to speed in no time, you don't need to become an expert — merely attempting to cut a short drama will help ramp up your storytelling skills.

Edit what? Here's a suggestion: Go to editstock.com and download one of their drama packages (I'd recommend *Home Alone* as it's mostly driven by images and juxtapositions). Cut it. Show people your cut. Get feedback, cut it some more. For a few dollars, you can upload it to Editstock for some expert feedback.

Be prepared to devote time to this. It's so worth it.

CHAPTER 11

WRITING IN THE CUTTING ROOM

Mashup, remix, and previsualization —
the screenwriter becomes editor

TO GET FROM THE WORD to the moving image, write the way editors cut. And, taking this a stage further, maybe the best place to do this is in the cutting room.

First, let's restate the premise of this for-the-cut argument: film is made in the edit suite. The edit suite is the final destination of our story. Screenwriter Frederick Palmer says:

> "We must, therefore, learn to put our dramatic action into picture form . . . Our schools are beginning to give definite training in visualization." (*Palmer Plan Handbook, Volume 1*)

Palmer is giving this advice to fellow screenwriters. Putting "our dramatic action into picture form" is the subject of this and the next couple of chapters.

In this world of digital plenty, it becomes increasingly possible for screenwriters to compose their stories in images and sounds. And here's the twist: Palmer is not a child of the digital age, he was a screenwriter from the silent era; this quote is from his manual published in 1922. He was from a generation of screenwriters, working at the film studio, fully immersed and skilled in production crafts. When he wrote his scripts, he visualized the beats, and prefigured the shoot and the edit.

As discussed in an earlier chapter, when the writing departments of the big studios closed, a new generation of screenwriters grew up outside "the factory," and they began using a screenplay format that got rid of the clutter of production descriptors. And that's where we are today. We quite like it out here; everyone's free to write a spec script, and yay we don't have to mess-up our stories with camera directions. We're also happy to write and write, knowing the chances of a green light is about the same as winning the lottery. (Man, what is wrong with us?!)

But this divorce from the studios has in some ways been deskilling; we have largely forgotten how to connect our writing to the production process. And screenwriting manuals give little help here.

All change. Today the world spins on a new digital axis, and surprisingly we find we can return to the film studios by a new route. We can immerse ourselves in virtual film sets and production processes; we can write with text, with images, and with sounds.

Dear writers let us mashup and remix. We're going to dive into the digital ocean, snaffle some tools from the edit suite, and cut our story.

OK, this is quite a jump. And why would we even want to do this?

Here are two ambitions:

1. If we were able to write using images, text, and sounds, then it's quite likely we'd deliver screenplays that sit much closer to the screen.

2. Just as editors are able to rehearse the cut, so we too might rehearse and "prove" our stories before the shoot begins.

And for any producers reading this book here's a third ambition:

3. Tighter scripts make big-budget savings, and no Monkey Time.

So this is a little experimental, but bear with me — it'll all come good.

Enter the cutting room

When you open a piece of editing software you find an array of digital tools for cutting the footage, color grading, and audio manipulation. Film clips are assembled in a timeline; each modification to the cut can be instantly replayed on screen. Cut by cut, the editor and director are testing the cinema-worthiness of their decisions. As already discussed, this is a kind of rapid prototyping where failure is a precondition of success. Samuel Beckett might have been talking about both writing and film editing when he wrote, "Ever tried. Ever failed. No matter. Try again. Fail again. Fail better." (*Worstward Ho*)

Both screenwriting and editing are iterative and mending crafts. Editors can "fail" quite rapidly, and so arrive at a good cut fairly quickly. Screenwriting on the other hand is all about slow failure. We're still using a typewriter.

When we look at other arts and crafts, we see most use prototyping as a method for perfecting design. A music composer rehearses a phrase of music on the piano before writing the orchestral score.

A sculptor will use a maquette. The architect has scale models and 3D animations.

How do screenwriters prototype their stories? The commonest methods are index cards and the "Board" (with some software equivalents). Occasionally writers will hold rehearsed readings — and this is a good thing, but rare. But all these approaches remain locked in the realm of words; the essential properties of cinema (kinesis, image, sound, fragment, and light) are nowhere in sight.

Back in the 1940s, when Eisenstein was writing *Ivan the Terrible*, he described a way of working that seems to hold great promise for us today:

> "When you are in a good working mood, images swarm through your busy imagination. Keeping up with them and catching them is very much like grappling with a run of herring. . . . You must drop your pencil and take up your pen to sketch the dialogue for this scene, and before the ink of this is dry, your pencil is once more making a note of an image that came to you during the dialogue . . . Whole scenes first take shape as batches of drawings before they take on the clothing of words." (*The Film Sense*)

One could argue Eisenstein isn't a regular kind of writer — he's also a director-producer so he would think that way wouldn't he? Here's the thing: we're all producers now.

We're all producers now

We live in the digisphere. To paraphrase some big cultural commentators — we have moved from an analog read-only culture to a digital read-write culture. We are the people "formerly known as the audience," digital producers able to make and mashup stories for YouTube, Vimeo, and the like. And production tools are available online and mostly free.

Now we can hatch our screen stories in new ways. As Lawrence Lessig, author of the seminal book *Remix Culture*, put it,

> "Writing with text is just one way to write, and not even the most interesting way to write. The more interesting ways are increasingly to use images and sound and video to express ideas" (*O'Reilly Network Policy DevCenter*)

If Palmer, Eisenstein, and the gang were writing scripts today, what digital tools and techniques would they reach for?

They'd be writing in the edit suite.

Of course, there's something a little provoking about the idea of writing in the edit suite. Editing is a postproduction craft, it comes into play after the script, and after the shoot. How can we writers possibly "cut" our story without rushes?

Well, we could use proxies. In the broadest sense, there's nothing revolutionary about using proxies to help tell our stories. And for some time now, a particularly useful way of simulating and testing cinema stories before the shoot is through use of previsualization (previs).

At the "high end," previs means animations generated in software such as Maya. Their purpose is to allow directors to rehearse technically complex chase-and-fight sequences for films like *Black Panther*. This kind of previs is expensive and doesn't in fact relate directly to storytelling. So let's not go there.

There's also a range of cheap or free previs tools designed for screenwriters to use. Some of these work like storyboards, others like animations. Some use a common stock of characters and settings, and presuppose an already formed story.

Some film directors have also experimented with these kinds of tools...

One from the heart

When I discussed the idea of screenwriters using previs with Walter Murch, he had a good cautionary tale. He recalled how previs nearly upended the filmmaking career of his longtime collaborator Francis Coppola. In 1980 Coppola had begun to prepare for his forthcoming musical film *One from the Heart*. Coppola invented a director's previs aid he called "electric cinema." This was a process for capturing and storyboarding sequences ahead of the shoot using drawings, audio recordings, videotape, and Polaroids. The fruits of this invention tend to justify Murch's skepticism: the story began life as a lean, black-and-white movie set in Chicago. After Coppola's electric cinema treatment, the story became a bloated, full color extravaganza set in Las Vegas. The shoot was so costly it nearly bankrupted his newly formed American Zoetrope company.

Screenwriting is a tight discipline, if you open the door to other media, your story could easily get lost in the traffic. And this is a legitimate concern.

But Coppola was experimenting in the pre-digital, pre Internet, pre-YouTube age. He was using equipment that was cutting edge for those analog times — audio recorders, VTRs, Polaroids, etc. This kit was cumbersome, and the media was slow and clunky to process. Time-jump to the twenty-first century, and it's a world of mostly-free software, where home computers open the door to a galaxy of media, editing software comes as standard, and you have the processing power to deliver cinema-scale movies.

Of course having software is not the same as having a craft; and most of us are not practiced editors. But the craft we do know is screenwriting, and when we open the "wrong" software and flex our storytelling muscle, new and exciting things can happen.

I did a survey . . .

I wanted to find out something of the habits of screenwriters. I was particularly interested to see if they ever used media in developing their stories. I surveyed 500 screenwriters, over 80 responded, and here's what I learned:

77% of us use pictures and sounds to develop our stories. But only 4% use any kind of audiovisual software.

This means that while most of us reach for pictures and sounds, we tend not to process these assets in a narrative sense. We're not "writing" with pictures and sounds using storytelling software; those assets are serving as stimuli, or mood references.

However, 65% declared an interest in using storytelling software.

Finally, 84% of writers expressed an interest in the idea of collaborative writing. I was quite surprised at this result; we know that screenwriting tends to be a solo activity, and we could be forgiven for thinking we like it that way. But it seems screenwriters do want to co-write, or maybe co-critique, and in fact 45% have already tried.

I asked this last question because cutting film is essentially a collaborative activity between editor and director. Few directors will actually sit and watch the editor cutting, but they will be engaged in an intense creative dialogue throughout the postproduction journey. With each new draft, editors will seek feedback from the director and sometimes the producer, and virtually anyone who strays into the edit suite. Sometimes just having someone in the room mutely watching can entirely refresh the editor's view of her work. Partly why editors seek this feedback is to help them combat iteration-fatigue. This is editor Mick Audsley on the subject:

"It's like reading the same poem over and over again . . . the meaning starts to erode and so to have a fresh viewpoint is difficult. The thing about film is it's shared, and all I can say is when you're getting particularly blind, if you sit someone down in the suite, and even if they say nothing, this odd thing happens: little sparks seem to come out of the pores of their skin and you start to think, 'Oh God, they're bored, or they're getting it, or they're excited or they're not,' and you just get it, and they don't have to have said a word — it's an odd chemistry."

And screenwriters are also reading the same poem over and over. Of course we too seek feedback from script readers, friends, and family. But these events occur only rarely, and usually at the final stages of the script.

CHAPTER 12

HATCHING THE STORY

*Writing with text, images, and sounds — the cut
tells the story, and the cut proves the story*

HIGH IN A DARK SKY, *a parachutist hovers under a vast thunderhead.
Then he disappears into the cloud. Lightning flashes silently.
A Glasgow tenement, loud rock music.
Jared is smoking on a balcony and jerking his limbs as if he's dancing
in his sleep.
Behind him TV news spills into a threadbare room.
"Police believe the youth is a BASE jumper and may have leapt from
the Sandy Heath radio mast in Bedfordshire . . ."
News footage shows villagers gathered round a lamppost.
Luke is unconscious and hanging by his chute strings.
His feet are bare.
Jared's eyes widen, seeing his brother on TV.
Thunder rolls.*

These are the opening beats of my screenplay *Rush the Sky*. When I
began work on this story, I wanted to write it for the cut. But I also
wanted to see to what degree I could write it "in the cutting room."

Screenwriters work in beats, and these beats are jigsaw pieces.

Could we make these beats behave like film clips, and could we mount them into sequences and make rough cuts? Film editor Eddie Hamilton says:

> "Generally speaking, the final structure of the movie doesn't reveal itself until you're editing. You often end up juggling scenes around — moving the Lego bricks on the timeline. Editing is writing and vice-versa."

And these are lyrics from a 1920s song, "'T'ain't No Sin" by Edgar Leslie and Walter Donaldson:

When you hear sweet syncopation
And the music softly moans
'T'ain't no sin to take off your skin
And dance about in your bones

When writing *Rush the Sky*, I wanted to do the Lego thing, and the dance thing. I wanted to reconfigure the parts, to dance the bones of my story and create new anatomies. And quickly.

So at first I literally went into the edit suite and gave it a go. It turns out working with captions and proxy images in editing software is actually a pain in the ass, and it can't show you anything much about story structure. I really needed a hybrid tool that was editor, word processor, and "the board."

I ended up using two apps: Scrivener and Prezi.

Ideally, this chapter should be a case study about someone who develops their screen story today the way Eisenstein did it back then. Someone like George Miller. We know he began his story for *Mad Max: Fury Road* by covering his wall with found images, and then developed the story as if it were a silent movie —

"The film was conceived visually. It was like a silent movie with sound and music . . . I definitely had the Hitchcock dictum in my head. He said, 'I try to make movies where they don't have to read the subtitles in Japan.' As it turned out, the Japanese really took to it." (*IndieWire*)

But·that's as much as I can tell you. I can't show how Miller worked with those images, structured them, how he developed the dialogue, and the screenplay. Because he said, "Hey — stop peeking in at my window!"

The way professional writers develop their stories is a secret; and the finished screenplay erases all trace of its construction. So I'm going to talk about *my* story. Clearly, it's not one you'll be familiar with — it's still a work-in-progress. But come in closer to the window . . .

Like this

Scrivener is essentially a super-agile word processing app, and it allowed me to compose my story in "jigsaw pieces"; I could then easily manipulate and revise my treatment in a nonlinear, unpaged manner. And in Prezi, I compressed these fragments into story beats and snatches of dialogue (like the beat poem at the top of this chapter). Then I attached them to proxy images and film clips from the web (Google images, Flickr, Bing, YouTube).

For those not familiar with Prezi, it's a zooming presentation tool; it gives you a boundless work surface on which to drag and drop all kinds of media. I designed a simple Three-Act Grid (like Blake Snyder's Board: Act 1, Act 2.1, Act 2.2, Act 3), and began mapping my story beats and images on to the grid. Rather like a film editor working in a timeline, I could rapidly "mount" and move my media fragments around, reconfigure sequences, play and replay.

It's hard to convey the kind of alchemy that now came into play. Just the simple process of reaching for images, clips, and sounds opened doors to worlds I could not have imagined. You could have no idea what harvest would be returned from your search terms. This is a bit like fishing on the Great Barrier Reef where you cast your net to catch snapper, and you do indeed catch snapper, but you also catch damselfish, clownfish, Wrasse, and things that are not even fish. This is what author and media thinker Steven Johnson calls the "adjacent possible." The web is a place of fabulous bounty and serendipity. Here, the interplay between fragments of text and my searches for proxy images and clips was truly generative.

> "Ideas are works of bricolage; they're built out of that detritus. We take the ideas we've inherited or that we've stumbled across, and we jigger them together into some new shape. We like to think of our ideas as $40,000 incubators, shipped direct from the factory, but in reality they've been cobbled together with spare parts that happened to be sitting in the garage." (*Where Good Ideas Come From*)

This principle of invention in the arts has a long history — probably we've been fooling around this way since cave art. Matisse offers a good model: his cut-outs were originally a way of prototyping his paintings. He made paper versions of the objects he wanted in his canvass so he could play with different compositions: let's put the Tahitian shell here, the apple over there and so on. Or think of William Burroughs and David Bowie using the cut-up techniques of Dada to compose stories and lyrics. And, of course, there's fridge magnet poetry. . . .

Dance the Bones

As I worked away, circulating the story between these two apps, writing "in the cutting room" became increasingly about structure.

Many "screenwriting gurus," such as Syd Field, Christopher Vogler, Blake Snyder, and John Truby, have suggested quite detailed structural maps of the Archetypal Movie. John Yorke, in his book *Into the Woods*, very usefully lines up a bunch of these archetypes in a single map, and astonishingly he reveals: they're all (more or less) the same!

Still, I remained rather skeptical about this. I can readily subscribe to the Three-Act model, but beyond that, it all looked a bit bogus.

But then I changed my mind after my experiments in Prezi. And it happened like this: I'm having fun moving the beats of my story around my Three-Act Grid. I'm color-coding my A and B plots and flashback moments, and what emerges is a structural map. And it looks surprisingly familiar.

I thought maybe I should look at Blake Snyder's beat sheet again — just for fun, you understand. Blake's beat sheet seemed particularly useful because it gives a suggested page number for each of his 15 beats, and so he's also giving you a time value ("Bad Guys Close In" happens from page 55 to 75 and so it comes between 55 to 75 minutes into the movie). So back to Prezi: I flagged these beats across my grid and I looked for the corresponding beats in my story. And well, they kind of match. But the bigger discovery was this: whatever beat sheet you use, and however ill-fitting it may seem, just having those big beats laid out is a graphic reminder of the need for your story to change, and oscillate, and keep moving forward.

Prezi is a motion environment; though quite crude (in a film-making sense), by simply clicking through the beats of my story, I was able to reproduce something of the kinetic, image, and time dimensions of cinema. I could play my story. The juxtapositions I was seeing created fresh storytelling possibilities as I continued to write my treatment in Scrivener.

And so the "editing" continued, until finally I was ready. I opened Final Draft.

It was at this screenplay stage that for-the-cut figures such as ellipsis, and "nonlinear shuffle" came into play. Here's an example: in one of the *Rush the Sky* scenes, our hero Luke is coaching Ella through a "tough love" fitness program over a period of months. Originally I'd written this as a banal music-and-montage sequence where we see Ella showing grit and anger and growing in strength (one of my script reader friends wittily called this my "*Rocky* moment"). Later I read the Karel Reisz discussion about script-planned montage, and I rewrote the scene and "intercut" this montage with fragments from several succeeding scenes: the lovers climbing a bridge span, playing hide-and-seek under a parachute, and watching the sky while Luke tells Ella about the clouds (sometimes in voiceover, and sometimes in picture). Through these juxtapositions, the sequence acquired a new subtext; Ella is growing in strength and falling love, but she is also being initiated into Luke's world of clouds and mortal dare.

Of course, as soon as you open Final Draft, you're back in the realm of words and white pages. Suddenly it looks like all the "cinema" you've simulated in Prezi is stripped out of the story. But actually, that beat phase carries forward into the screenwriting because as you write, you're capturing in words all the vivid worlds, events, and characters you've seen with your own eyes. And the story should be strong, because in some measure, you've proved it for cinema.

Exercises

Make one of these. Use Prezi or PowerPoint or Adobe Spark or whatever works for you. Search using Google Images, Flickr, or Bing. You'll probably find it gets quite difficult to build a whole screen story this way, but you can certainly have fun composing scenes and sequences.

CHAPTER 13

ART OF THE MAGPIE

How to make a sizzler

THIS CHAPTER IS about sizzle reels. If you've travelled with me this far, and you've already experimented with writing with text and pictures, and done some editing like I told you, then what happens next is the thing that must happen next. And even if you've never edited before, you can learn the basics and cut your first "mood sizzler" in a day. Of course, it will be crap first try.

A sizzle reel is a magpie trailer for a film that doesn't yet exist. It shows the story idea, the style, and the world of the screenplay using a cunning patchwork of found footage, specially recorded voiceovers, text, sound effects, and music. Producers who have a hot screenplay and want to attract investment often commission sizzlers.

But we're not making one of those yet. So, unlike the producer's selling sizzler, you're making one to rehearse your story idea, to get a sense of what it looks like when you get it up on its feet and give it the breath of life. Something you can show to people, and get feedback.

The process of making your sizzler keeps your story in the world of pictures and sounds and cinema. It obliges you to find films that are like yours, and really understand the genre of your screenplay. You will comb films for likely actors to play the roles you've written (which can be a huge help in terms of character development and dialogue later on). And you will search for your big cinematic scores, you will record dialogue (you and your friends), and make some decisions about style and look. You will do it all, in your front room, on your computer. This is "skint cinema."

What do they look like?

If you go online and hunt down sizzle reels, you'll find a ragtag of previews, lazy montages, computer game ads, behind-the-scenes schlock, showreels, and corporate cha-cha. You're unlikely to find a serious "selling sizzler" because obviously these are password-protected (they're brimful of copyright material, so if they were published they'd be taken down in a blink). The only reason I've seen so many is because I know a company that makes them for a living.

The exception to the rule is the *Looper* sizzler. A lot of people know about this because it's virtually the only example currently available online. And it's excellent. It was uploaded by *Looper* director Rian Johnson, and it seems no one's told him to take it down. This is what he says:

> "Just after I finished the script for *Looper*, but before we began preproduction, I asked Joe to record some voiceover, and with help from my friend Ronen Verbit constructed this 'fake trailer' using clips from other movies. This is a fairly common thing to do when you're trying to get a movie off the ground, but it was the first time I tried it. It was meant to show more some of the film's tone, and to show how the odd concept could be presented in a clear and compelling way in the marketing." (Go to Vimeo or YouTube and search for *Looper clip-o-matic trailer.*)

After you've watched the sizzler, look at the official film trailer for *Looper* — the similarity will blow your socks off.

So *Looper* is a great example. It's such an impressive statement of intent that everyone can see and understand the idea from the director to the actor, to the carpenter. Johnson was never going to get a torpedo boat.

For something a little more ambient, you might want to check out the "pitch reel" for *The Hunger Games* by director Kevin Tancharoen (currently on the *No Film School* website). With a running time of over 4 minutes, it's quite long for a sizzler, but genius in the way Tancharoen has found sync dialogue from a slew of great action movies and confected the distinctive world of the *Hunger Games*.

Looking at these examples, you might be thinking this sizzle thing is only for action movies. It's not — doesn't matter if you're writing a romcom, a drama, a biopic, or a horror film, the principle is the same.

When to sizzle your story

Any time, from first glimmer, to full treatment, to final draft. With the first glimmer, you'd be making a "mood sizzler," a kind of ambient montage of found footage and music. At the treatment phase, the sizzler can start to resemble the shape of a trailer and may include snatches of dialogue. And with the more finished screenplay, you'd be making a "looper." Hope that's clear.

Plan to spend a solid week on this. If you're coming fresh to editing, be prepared for a lot of repetition, frustration, and failure. But also be prepared for magic. You're remixing the world of film — throwing together clips from wildly different sources — and these fresh associations will unleash the wonders of juxtaposition, of haiku, of serendipity.

You are using the sizzler as a kind of diagnostic tool. So once you've made your first one, you need to organize a test screening. Gather a small posse of friends and family in front of a big TV, pass round the popcorn, and show them what you've got. Do a Q&A, and gather the feedback. At heart, this is a high-octane elevator pitch.

No one's written the book of sizzle

So how do you do it? We begin with a close examination of how a film trailer works. A trailer is intended to sell the story idea of the movie. The story idea builds out from the logline, and contains some of the actual story, makes clear the genre, who's the hero, who's the villain, the set up, and it gives glimpses of the big set pieces. It shows you the actors of course. How much of the story should be in there? Just enough to create puzzle and excitement. Bad trailers tell you everything.

Trailers are a compressed form. Every shot, every sound effect, every piece of music, every word of dialogue and voiceover is precision engineered to ramp up suggestion, puzzle, and kinesis. Even if you were a professional editor, you're unlikely to make a brilliant trailer unless you cut trailers and promos for a living. This storytelling form has its own cinematic shorthand, a shorthand that continues to evolve over the years and dances tantalizingly one step faster than the smartest person in the room.

But the good news is this: you're not actually making a film trailer, you're making a proof-of-concept sizzler. And you can jump into this thing with only a basic understanding of editing. You just need to embrace "getting it wrong," and be open to discovery.

Get ready. You're going to download Vimeo and YouTube clips, rip DVDs, and plunder the wild riches of the Internet. Be a mad and shameless magpie. But unless your name is Rian Johnson or Kevin Tancharoen, do not put any of it online.

EXERCISE 1: REVERSE-ENGINEER A TRAILER

A good place to start is to tease out the DNA of commercial film trailers. How do they work? You're about to discover this in a very practical way.

Make a shortlist of movies that are like your screenplay. Then check the trailers for those films. Double-check this, you may find that the film is right, but the trailer is wrong for your purposes. You want a model that is right film and right trailer.

Download the trailers that best fit. And now you can get into the forensics.

Open your editing software, import the clip, and drop it into your timeline.

So this trailer runs maybe 90 to 150 seconds, and through the process of reverse engineering, you are going to make visible all the cuts that are now invisible in this "flattened" version sitting in your timeline. Reverse-engineering is simply the mechanical process of making the cuts visible.

Deselect the two audio channels (you're going to leave these alone), and then find the tool that allows you to "add edit." Press play and pause the play head at the first "flattened" cut. Now add edit, and move to the next cut. Repeat for the entire trailer. That's a lot of edits, but it's only a mechanical operation so shouldn't take too long. (In some more sophisticated software you'll find a function called "scene detect" and this automatically adds edit at every cut.)

Now you're looking at the video track with all the cuts, just as the original trailer editor saw it. Time to begin your investigation; see how it moves — understand its construction. Trailers will often break into three acts (though they can sometimes come in two or four act flavors). And the demarcation of the act is very often signaled by a change of music. How does your trailer break down? Can you describe the music? Is it fast, mid-tempo, slow? What are the featured instruments, is it a big orchestral piece, vocals, or minimalist? Look at the cutting pattern, are there sections where there are clusters of short clips, or longer clips? Is there much continuity going on, or is it fragmentary, jumpy, and juxtaposition-y? Is the "hard information" carried by voiceover, dialogue, or captions — or all three? Write a transcript of every word spoken on screen and in voiceover; this alone will reveal so much about the art of trailers. What else is happening on the soundtrack? Appreciate the layering of the sound effects. Figure out why they don't use music for some sections. How much of the story is revealed, how much concealed. How are they creating puzzle and traction? Really rinse this thing — the more you look, the more you'll discover. You are learning magic.

EXERCISE 2: MAKE A MOOD SIZZLER

This will get you started. It runs between 30 and 100 seconds. Go find film clips from full-length movies that chime with your story in terms of genre, world of your story, look, atmosphere, maybe actors.

Next, choose lots of contrasting music tracks that seem to resonate with the different moods of your story (you can also experiment with pieces that work against the grain of your story to create a sense of unease or irony).

Edit sections of the music into the timeline (let's say 10 seconds of an up-tempo piece, 25 seconds of a mid-tempo piece, and 10 seconds of a fast piece). The music will serve as the "driver" in the selection of your film clips and the pace of your edit.

Now start cutting pictures — you're going to make a montage

(avoid too much cutting on rhythm, you're not making a music video). You may want to strip out most of the synchronous sound and just let the images, the action, the look, the choreography, and the music do their work — but be alive to the possibility that some of the sync dialogue can enormously enrich your sequence (sometimes dialogue can prove particularly effective when used as voiceover narration across entirely unrelated images).

Find clips that suggest the dynamics and structure of your story. Don't spend too much time choosing a specific actor to play your hero or villain — enjoy the fact that your hero may be played by a different actor in almost every shot. This is a mood piece, you're working in broad brushstrokes, so don't get hung up on creating any kind of continuity (the music will bind all these disparate clips together anyway). Work in fragments, create juxtapositions, and prick the curiosity of the viewer.

EXERCISE 3: CREATE A LOOPER SIZZLER

Runs 100 seconds. This is your fake trailer.

In prospect, it may seem that a sizzler containing a galaxy of faces and locations from different films is going to be really confusing for the viewer — how will they even know who's the hero and who's the villain? But *Looper* demonstrates how a sharply written voiceover, placed alongside images, juxtapositions, and good sound design, can homogenize differences and deliver a clear idea.

A good starting point for your looper sizzler is the logline, because the logline contains the essence of your story idea, and it will keep you anchored.

You will need to write a short script which will be carried by any combination of the following: voiceover narrator (you), some characters (you again, and some of your friends), captions (don't get fancy — stick to white out of black).

It's worth revisiting all the fundamental questions every screen-writer should want the viewer to understand: who is the hero, what is his / her mission. What "gifts" or "powers" do they have, or want to possess. Who is the villain / impediment? What is the jeopardy? Where is the story set? What does the world of the story look like (key locations)? What is the conflict? What is the twist?

And when you sit down to write this sizzle script, consider how much of this the audience needs to know through "hard informa-tion" (i.e., voiceover, dialogue, and captions), and how much can be inferred through "soft information" (i.e., choice of images, jux-tapositions, sound effects, music).

Then consider which model you prefer. Johnson's *Looper* is a first person narrative; it goes like this:

> "Time travel has not been invented. But in 30 years it will be —
> it will be very illegal, used only by large criminal groups. My
> employers. When they need someone in the future to disappear,
> they grab him, zap him back in time, to me — so he vanishes
> from the future, and I kill a man who does not yet exist. Assassins
> like me are called 'loopers' — we shoot fish in a barrel. We are
> well paid. We live the good life, while the world crumbles around
> us. And the only rule is — when the man appears — you pull the
> trigger. Easy. Until a man appeared who was me."

Very possibly your screenplay contains no voiceovers what-soever and you might quickly dismiss this model. But it doesn't matter, because a sizzler is quite a different beast from a film. So imagine your protagonist were explaining the set up to a friend. What would that sound like?

Another very common model is to use snatches of suggestive dialogue from various characters. This is *Ghost in the Shell* — there's maybe four different characters here:

"I have been watching you."
"You have to remember."
"I saw someone down there."
"He's a known terrorist and he's killed again."
"Didn't just kill them — they hacked into their minds."
"He's everywhere and nowhere."
"I will find him. And I will kill him."

Or you could do most of the work with captions. Here's my sizzle script for *Rush the Sky* (everything in quotes is a voiceover, and the rest are captions).

Boy meets girl
And they climb into the sky
"How did you even do that?"
"Some death on your tongue girl, and you know you're alive."
Here comes the Mad Squad
"Your boy Archer's been cutting the food?"
"Head in the fucking clouds that's your trouble"
"Tell them to stop!"
Wake up
"Look at me love, please look at me."
Dare to fight
Dare to love
Wake up
Rush the sky

Look at the economy and apparent simplicity of the trailer for *Jackie*. The "hard information" contains zero exposition — she's talking about Camelot and believing in fairytales.

"People like to believe in fairytales
Don't let it be forgot — that once there was a spot
That for one brief shining moment
There was a Camelot
There won't be another Camelot, not another Camelot"

The words acquire an enormous emotional charge as the music wells up and we see images of the Kennedys' glamorous life together, his bloody assassination, and her grief. This is the poetry of cinema.

Tips

When it comes to editing, whether you're a novice or a ninja, aim to cut your first draft quite rapidly. Don't get precious about the ordering or the exact duration of your clips — just lay it down and get to the finishing post. Screenwriters will be familiar with a similar process we call the "vomit draft." Writing is rewriting, and editing is reediting.

Even if your screen story is entirely linear, your trailer might be more effective as a "shuffle." For example, some trailers swap act two and three so that the trailer ends on the big turning point at the end of act two.

Don't attempt to tell your story in 100 seconds — you want to seduce the audience, arouse their appetite for more.

Add sound effects where it feels useful to help tell the story, or in raising the emotional temperature of the piece. Dogs barking, waves lapping on a shore, wind blowing . . . and, of course, guns, car crashes, helicopters, explosions, whooshes, drones, humming, ticking, etc. Check out the world of free sound effects online.

If you don't like the sound of your own voice or the voices of any of your friends — use one of the online freelance sites like *fiverr* where voiceover artists will record your lines for a small fee. (Good voiceover artists may be able to do two or three different voices for you.)

Your sizzler should have a fairly wild cardiogram, and move along at markedly different tempos. Your choice of music is going to help with this. But also allow juxtaposition to do its job.

Keep in mind this is about process, not product; the process should be revealing things to you. After your first screening, gather the feedback, make another cut, and show it again. And again. As we've said before, the thing with rapid prototyping is it's a process of perfection through failure.

Don't go looking for source clips without a plan. You'll get lost and waste most of your precious young life.

CHAPTER 14

WAY STATION

Nearly a conclusion

We're still learning about the cut. Maybe we'd learn a lot more if screenwriters and a film editor were talking to each other: but you'll rarely find them in the same room. They sit at the head and tail of a process, and they're seemingly worlds apart. But the fact is we're all storytellers, and I believe technology is drawing us closer together.

During the course of my research, I've had to change some of my ideas. There really is an awful lot of waste in film production, and I imagined tighter scripts would be one of the big prizes of *writing for the cut*. We know that from the initial rough cut to the final cut, a film will typically lose up to thirty percent of its body mass. Of course, some of this will be baggy editing, but that thirty percent also means lots of dialogue, whole scenes, and sometimes entire subplots, will end up on the "cutting room floor." And this is true of every genre of film.

For sure, *writing for the cut* will reduce some of that story wastage, but I've come to appreciate this is a really a complex field; all editors I interviewed expected a healthy narrative surplus from which to sculpt the story and to fix problems. An early draft of *The English Patient* came in at four and a half hours. Editor Walter Murch says, "The screenplay generated the material that allowed you as the tailor to turn this pair of trousers into a dress."

But what is a healthy surplus? And would an editor need less if the script were better designed for the cut? There is a species of film that produces virtually zero narrative waste in postproduction: animation. There are good reasons for this extraordinary economy. Very often writing and storyboarding progress in tandem. And later, every moment, every detail is choreographed and tested using animatics before going into full production. Animated stories are tight, tight, tight. Of course live action movies cannot be nearly so controlled. Nevertheless, perhaps we can learn much by examining the way Pixar tests their stories before going into production.

One of the biggest casualties in the edit suite is dialogue. But this sometimes turns out to be a necessary casualty; the lines are there to give the actor emotional clues. The actor can say the lines, and because she understands the intention, she can also deliver the "I love you" look that, in the edit suite, makes not only the lines redundant, but perhaps the next two scenes beyond.

I want to finish here with an image from the film *Trumbo*. Set during McCarthy-era America, it's a biopic about the lefty screenwriter Dalton Trumbo (*Spartacus, Exodus, Roman Holiday*). I like this image so much — it shows the man working in the bath, cutting up his script, adding and subtracting, moving the parts around, and keeping the story in motion.

POSTSCRIPT

In an earlier chapter, I wrote about my experiments "writing in the cutting room" using Scrivener and Prezi. For me, using software in this way was a revelation. On the downside, these apps are clearly not for the purpose. A feature film is a big piece of work, and the bigger your project, the more unwieldy and laggy the process.

I have a digital dream. I'm developing a web app for screenwriters to create and test their stories. This app gives you a work surface like Prezi, a timeline like a film editor's, a structural view like "the board," and a treatment view like nobody's business. And it'll give you real-time collaboration with other writers and reviewers.

If this interests you, come and find me online — we need to talk.

FURTHER READING

Here's a short selection of sources that have helped shape this book.

Apple, Wendy. *The Cutting Edge: The Magic of Movie Editing.* Warner Home Video, 2005.

Chang, Justin. *FilmCraft: Editing.* Waltham, Mass.: Focal Press, 2012.

Eisenstein, Sergei. *The Film Sense.* Houghton Mifflin Harcourt, 1969.

Hitchcock, Alfred. *Hitchcock / Truffaut.* Simon and Schuster, 1985.

Mackendrick, Alexander. *On Film-Making.* Ed. Paul Cronin. London: Faber & Faber, 2006.

Mamet, David. *On Directing Film.* New York. London: Penguin, 1992.

Murch, Walter. *In the Blink of an Eye, Revised 2nd Edition.* Silman-James Press, 2001.

Ondaatje, Michael. *The Conversations: Walter Murch and the Art of Editing Film.* Bloomsbury Publishing plc, 2009.

Rosenblum, Ralph, and Robert Karen. *When the Shooting Stops . . . the Cutting Begins: A Film Editor's Story.* New Ed edition. New York: Da Capo Press, 1986.

ABOUT THE AUTHOR

 **GREG LOFTIN** is a screenwriter who in 2007 wrote and directed his feature film, the award-winning urban western *Saxon*.

His extensive research for *Writing for the Cut* forms the basis of his Ph.D which he completed in 2016 at the University of Exeter.

He lectures at Ravensbourne University London where he his course leader of the first undergraduate programme in Editing and Post Production in the UK.

Through his world class program of editor master classes, he was able to gather many of the vital insights for this book from the likes of Walter Murch (*Apocalypse Now, The Godfather*), Paul Machliss (*Scott Pilgrim vs. the World, Baby Driver*) Tom Rolf (*Taxi Driver, Heat*), Mick Audsley (*Harry Potter and the Goblet of Fire, Murder on the Orient Express*), and Lisa Gunning (*Nowhere Boy, Seven Psychopaths*).

{ THE MYTH OF MWP }

In a dark time, a light bringer came along, leading the curious and the frustrated to clarity and empowerment. It took the well-guarded secrets out of the hands of the few and made them available to all. It spread a spirit of openness and creative freedom, and built a storehouse of knowledge dedicated to the betterment of the arts.

The essence of the Michael Wiese Productions (MWP) is empowering people who have the burning desire to express themselves creatively. We help them realize their dreams by putting the tools in their hands. We demystify the sometimes secretive worlds of screenwriting, directing, acting, producing, film financing, and other media crafts.

By doing so, we hope to bring forth a realization of 'conscious media' which we define as being positively charged, emphasizing hope and affirming positive values like trust, cooperation, self-empowerment, freedom, and love. Grounded in the deep roots of myth, it aims to be healing both for those who make the art and those who encounter it. It hopes to be transformative for people, opening doors to new possibilities and pulling back veils to reveal hidden worlds.

MWP has built a storehouse of knowledge unequaled in the world, for no other publisher has so many titles on the media arts. Please visit www.mwp.com where you will find many free resources and a 25% discount on our books. Sign up and become part of the wider creative community!

Onward and upward,

Michael Wiese
Publisher/Filmmaker